MALCOLM WELLS

# The Earth-Sheltered House

## AN ARCHITECT'S SKETCHBOOK

Chelsea Green Publishing Company

White River Junction, Vermont

Printed in the United States of America.

00 99 98   1 2 3 4 5

First Chelsea Green edition printed September, 1998

Library of Congress Cataloging-in-Publication Data available by request.

CHELSEA GREEN PUBLISHING COMPANY
P.O. Box 428
White River Junction, Vermont 05001
www.chelseagreen.com

"Underground? Who, me? Are you kidding? I don't want to live like a mole. I'll be underground long enough when I'm dead."

How many times have I heard those words! Thousands. How many times have I responded? Thousands. Even though I've known that few people would be persuaded until they'd actually stepped into a building covered with wildflowers. "Underground" made them think of dark subways, leaky basements, and mildewed crawl spaces. They had every right to be skeptical.

What I like best are their reactions to the real thing: "It's so bright in here!" "I love the silence!" "Is this air conditioned?" This last is the question most often asked on those hot, July days when the change from hot and humid to dry and cool almost takes people's breath away. The underground prejudices dissolve instantaneously.

But I didn't become an underground architect for those reasons. I did it because we're so quickly paving everything with buildings and asphalt. I became an underground architect because it's the only way to build without destroying land.

It works. It really works. And, in addition to having a green "footprint," every underground building is also

silent,
bright,
dry,
sunny,
long-lasting,
easy to maintain,
easy to heat and cool,
and fire-safe.

Think about that.

—MALCOLM WELLS

**4**

When I was just a little squirt, growing up in New Jersey, I saw, every Sunday, in the town of Cedarbrook, a strange concrete structure. It was just one of the many things I came to know on the way to my grandparents' house.

Not till I was grown up, and an architect, did it occur to me that that strange structure was anything really special.

How had a Wrightian-cantilevered-reinforced-concrete pedestal come to a tiny village in a farm community? How had plants appeared on top of it? How did they survive? Who built it? And when?

I don't know if the structure is still there. I don't want to find out. It's very likely to have been swept away, along with the town itself, in the tidal wave of suburban sprawl around Philadelphia.

Somewhere between the two, between the suburban sprawl and the graceful plant-covered structure, the idea of a gentler kind of architecture found its way into my head, but it took its own sweet time in getting there. I had been a practicing architect for 11 years before I began to wonder if there was something less destructive than asphalt and concrete and toxic green lawns.

Marguerite Kinniey Wells got started in '95 and is still going strong. She's always been my favorite mother, so, as a token of my love, I hereby dedicate almost this whole page just to her. Ma, can you read all this tiny print?

The answer, of course, was all around me. The natural world teemed with examples. That the surface of the earth was meant for living plants, instead of dead buildings and asphalt, never got through to me until the environmental consciousness of the sixties unclogged my head. That's when the earth-cast buildings of Riviera architect Jacques Couelle, the strange pedestal in New Jersey, and Frank Lloyd Wright's underground theatre got together and decided it was time for me to wake up.

In 1959, at Taliesin West, I stepped out of the hot desert sunlight into this little open-to-the-air theatre, and marveled for a moment or two at Mr. Wright's genius, his ability to carry a design through into the tiniest of details, before it struck me that I was suddenly cool and comfortable there under a mantle of earth.

It took me only 5 more years to get the message. In 1964, I suddenly had a brilliant and original idea: buildings should be underground!

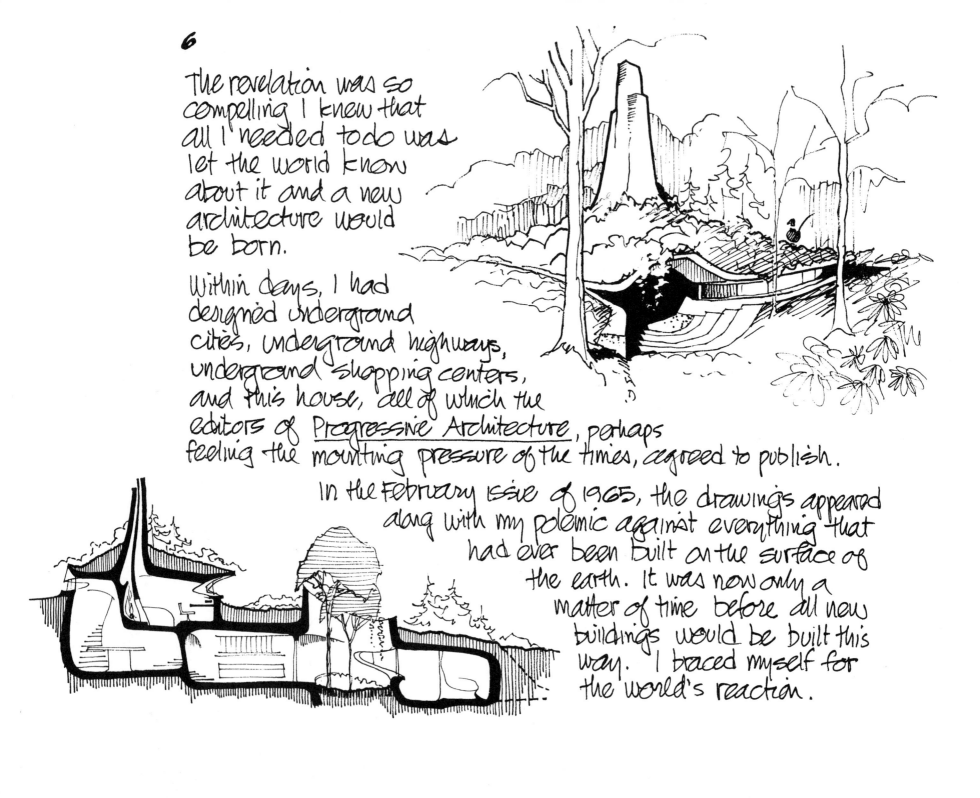

The revelation was so compelling I knew that all I needed to do was let the world know about it and a new architecture would be born.

Within days, I had designed underground cities, underground highways, underground shopping centers, and this house, all of which the editors of Progressive Architecture, perhaps feeling the mounting pressure of the times, agreed to publish.

In the February issue of 1965, the drawings appeared along with my polemic against everything that had ever been built on the surface of the earth. It was now only a matter of time before all new buildings would be built this way. I braced myself for the world's reaction.

The world, it appeared, had other fish to fry. A hundred letters and a few lecture dates were all that came of it — except for the reaction to this house.

It was, and still is, the most popular of all my underground designs, even though, to my knowledge, no one has ever built it, and, even if he did, it would have to be built entirely by hand and would take years to build.

There's something about the earth-relatedness of these free-form spaces that seems to tug at a lot of us, just as the Couelle designs, from which I borrowed so much of this one, tugged at me.

I use its appeal to convince myself that we have more than an intellectual interest in getting closer to the flowering earth. I think our roots are in it, too.

FIRE

LIVING ROOM, BELOW

DOWN

STUDY

ENTR. PATHS

DOWN

BED ROOM 3  BED ROOM 2  BATH  BATH  BED ROOM 1

GARDEN ENTRANCE

One result of the P.A. article was a commission for this house in Cherry Hill, New Jersey, my home town from 1949 till 1977, when it had become so bad I had to flee.

Mr. and Mrs. Lem, the clients, were generous in their reactions to the design but the land purchase didn't go through and the project be-

These were to be classrooms at an environmental center in South Jersey's wet, low cranberry country. "Sorry, no funds," said the state.

And you'll read all about this little chapel when you get to page 19.

→ came an orphan. It was the first of many orphans growing out of that article....

I didn't know, in 1965, that ice pressures in rooftop soil could crack retaining walls, causing all kinds of leaks and structural damage. Fortunately for all concerned, I found out the easy way, by reading about it, so this Mansard-façaded roof-garden building never had a chance to embarrass me. (It was never built.)

I had been sure that my developer friend, Bob Scarborough, would leap at the chance to pile tons of earth on top of his new office building, even though no one of his acquaintance — or mine either, for that matter — had ever built anything like it before.

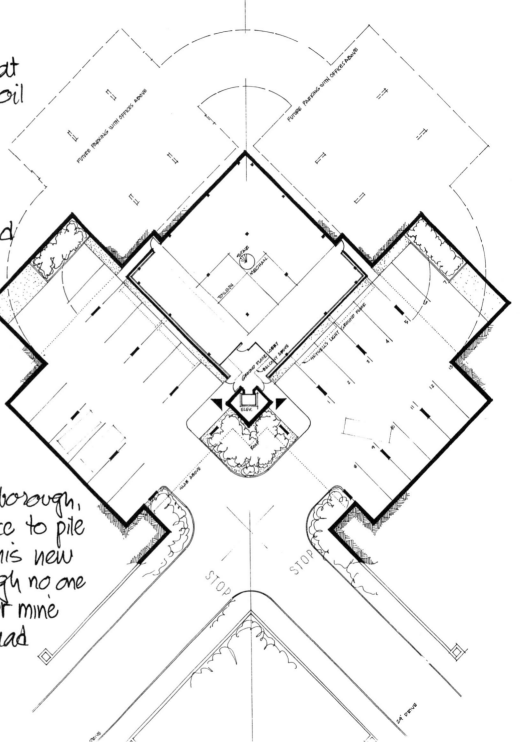

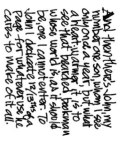

Bob was too smart to fall into a trap like that. He paid me and thanked me for my efforts and built a conventional structure that served him and his growing staff well for many years.

As is obvious from a glance at this design, the ideas of heat loss and of solar energy had not yet entered my consciousness.

It was just another exercise in testing the possibilities of building in the earth, and, as such, it probably was of some value to me.

This cross-section

is an invitation to disaster — thermal, structural, and fluvial, not to mention architectural... a wasteful above-ground building dragged, against its will, into the mud of south Jersey.

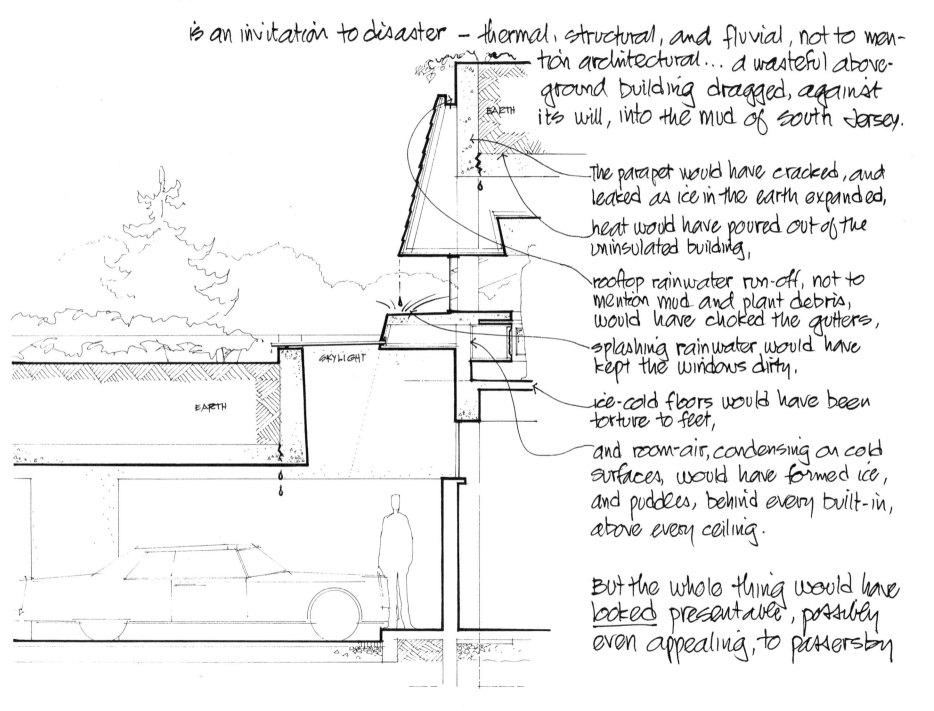

EARTH

SKYLIGHT

EARTH

The parapet would have cracked, and leaked as ice in the earth expanded,

heat would have poured out of the uninsulated building,

rooftop rainwater run-off, not to mention mud and plant debris, would have choked the gutters,

splashing rainwater would have kept the windows dirty.

ice-cold floors would have been torture to feet,

and room-air, condensing on cold surfaces, would have formed ice, and puddles, behind every built-in, above every ceiling.

But the whole thing would have looked presentable, possibly even appealing, to passersby unaware of the internal flaws. The then-in-style Mansard roofs, the great planters, and the horizontality of the lines (in contrast to the growing jumble of competing horrors along the highways) might have been judged acceptable, in that way beginning to

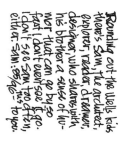

institutionalize a whole family of design that needed far more study before edging its way into the architectural mainstream.

Lyndon Johnson was president, and roadside beauty was the only issue that even came close to being an environmental one. Gasoline and oil were cheap. And a faraway war in the jungles of Asia was just starting to trouble us. We were still living back in the Fifties.

The mounting problems of waste and pollution exemplified by the American way of life, the destruction of wildlife habitat, the threat of nuclear power, the plight of black people and other minorities, the energy "cost" of materials, the erosion of America's farmsoil, the suffering of starving people, even the idea of harmful food additives... these and a score of other issues so well-known to us today were known to few of us in the mid-60$^s$.

Only after failing for years to see it, did I finally awaken to the damage that buildings do to living land. Of all the other problems I was as

Reaching out the Wells kids there's Sam, the architect, explorer, reader, dreamer, designer, who shares with his brother a sense of humor that can go by so fast I don't even see it go. I don't see Sam too often, either. Sam: This I give to you.

innocent as a newborn babe.

Thank god for subtle influences! Because of my underground proposals I was starting to correspond with, and to meet, men and women who were able to see the big picture and to transmit a little of it to me.

Solar energy! What a great idea!
Percolation beds!
Composting wastes!
Natural landscapes!

In 1969, the American Association of Museums convened a gathering of great environmentalists like me (hee hee) to deal with the ways in which the museums of America could transmit the environmental mess —and message— to the public. There I was, sitting in a huge conference room in New York, listening to eminent ecologists, biologists, naturalists, and museum directors discuss issues that seemed to have immense relevance for architecture. I could feel a whole new type of design swelling up inside of me, producing as its first fruit this "Museum of the Future" as the centerpiece of our

report. The idea was that by exhibiting these things outwardly, museums could say, at a glance, that a new land ethic was here.

The report generated a lot of design commissions. The first was a solar village on the south face of a great mesa in southern Colorado. Almost totally self-sufficient, this complex of solar hillside earth shelters was to have been reached by means of a covered escalator or tramway, up from the cars parked at river level. And then: poof! It all disappeared as the backers of the project turned to other matters and the momentum was lost.

A similar poof! was this invitation to design a headquarters building for the national park at Big Bend, Texas. You can see more details in my 1977 book, Underground Designs (see page 191), but this drawing tells perhaps all that need be told: reverence for, rather than domination of the earth, a sentiment now more strongly expressed by the Earth First! movement.

Meanwhile, back in New Jersey, interest, if not budgets, was growing, spurred by the activities of Earth Day '70.

I wasn't at all sure that solar heating was practical but the people I respected said it was, so I continued to propose it whenever I designed an earth-covered building.

This was to have been the headquarters of yet another New Jersey land developer, a change-of-pace building at which, once the visitor had driven in through the high mound of earth along the highway, he would be in another world, cut off from highway noises and ugliness, in an emerging natural landscape.

It might have gone ahead, but then his whole operation was moved to Washington.

As the seventies began to unfold and energy prices inched upward, things like solar energy and improved insulation began to get more serious consideration. It was not an unalloyed blessing, for it played to our emerging "me-generation" selfish-ness. Gentle Architecture was being accepted for less-than-altruistic reasons, and the underlying environmental motive was forgotten, forgotten so completely that it is now just starting to reassert itself, once more for perhaps the wrong reasons.

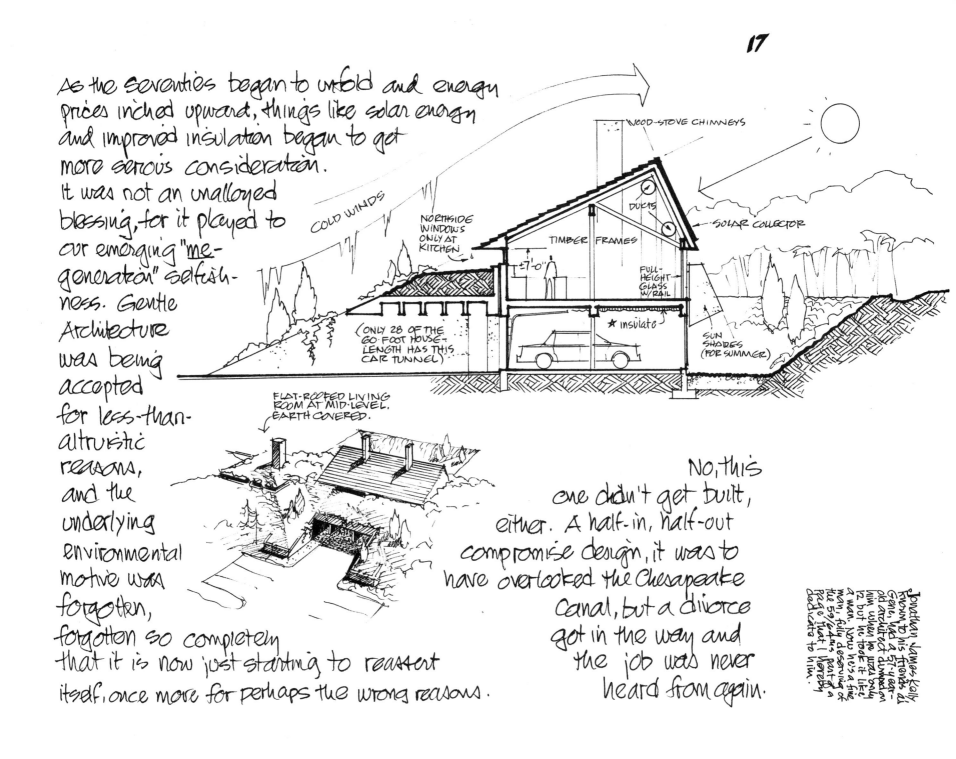

WOOD-STOVE CHIMNEYS

COLD WINDS

NORTHSIDE WINDOWS ONLY AT KITCHEN

DUCTS

TIMBER FRAMES

SOLAR COLLECTOR

±7'-0"

FULL-HEIGHT GLASS W/RAIL

* insulate

SUN SHADES (FOR SUMMER)

(ONLY 28 OF THE 60-FOOT HOUSE-LENGTH HAS THIS CAR TUNNEL)

FLAT-ROOFED LIVING ROOM AT MID-LEVEL, EARTH COVERED.

No, this one didn't get built, either. A half-in, half-out compromise design, it was to have overlooked the Chesapeake Canal, but a divorce got in the way and the job was never heard from again.

Jonathan James Kelly, known to his friends as Gene, was a 57-year-old architect dumped on him when he was only 12 but he took it like a man. Now he's a fine man, fully deserving of the 59 letters, I penta Page that I hereby dedicate to him.

You probably never even heard of The Great Environmental coloring Book of Life and Death and Architecture, did you?

Self-published in 1971, it was used as my platform, for a while, to present a lot of the ideas that weren't getting used in the real world of envionmental architecture.

No one, apparently, ever used it as a coloring book but it did fall into some good hands, generating a bit of this new architecture... A percolation bed here, some natural landscaping there...

I can see now that these first two sketches came from a) the winning design for Boston's city hall, and b) the heliport at the 1964 New York World's fair. Number three came from our growing interest in the plight of the poor — mostly black- people — trapped in the worst parts of dying cities. They were — and are — forced to breathe the worst of our air and drink the worst of our water.

Out beyond the suburbs, where the air and the water were still relatively clean, a group of businessmen raising money for a Boy Scout camp chapel actually went for the idea of covering its roof with earth as an expression of reverence for life. The idea was publicized, money was raised, and plans were drawn, but when it was decided that the scouts themselves should build the structure the roof was changed to one of logs, 2x4s, and plywood, and the design was diluted beyond recognition. Whether the scouts themselves had any part in the decision-making process was never revealed to me. I do know that the percolation-bed floor of the chapel was abandoned, asphalt or concrete being the replacement.

Well, there's plenty of percolation out in the woods. It was more for a gesture than for a need. It's in built-up areas, where the run-off from buildings and parking lots can get into 30,000-gallon quantities (for every impervious acre involved during a 1" rainstorm) that water conservation measures are so badly needed.

PERCOLATION BED

Two more pages of sketches from the coloring book... the subject here: entering the earth; how you go about doing it appropriately. It shouldn't be like walking into the shopping center or the bank. It should be, somehow, an act of humility.

The wild creatures of the earth know how to do this. Their entrances, while created, admittedly, for defense, have an appropriateness we have never matched. When _we_ build entrances designed primarily for defense they look even more forbidding and destructive than our conventional entrances, which are bad enough.

These 3 sketches were done as design proposals for a state park visitors' center in Pennsylvania. Building a naturalistic-looking entrance that wouldn't invite all sorts of leak, dirt, rodent, and security troubles would be a challenge, as would the idea of creating something that didn't look as fake as some "natural" buildings in zoos.

Stewart Rawling's Mott has been my son for only 2 years and yet he's a dad over 50. (How can that be?) This super-smart man of so many interests has a giant chunk of this page, now, in his name, which I believe you already know.

There was talk, in the early 70s, of building a huge jetport in New Jersey's "Pine Barrens", the forest that covers much of the center of the state. There was talk of square <u>miles</u> of rooftop and paving areas, and of what the run-off from so many chemicals would do to the forest's aquifer from which so many New Jerseyans drink. My proposal for a jetport at which everything but the runways was underground cut the paved areas by almost 90%. But then the state stepped in and bought the Pine Barrens as a conservation area and the great underground airport was no more. How long the state will hold out in the face of development pressure pinching it on both sides, from Philadelphia and Atlantic City, is an open question.

Another nature center that never got going, was this. It had a rooftop pond and stood in a pebbled courtyard.

A few months later, realizing it was time to put up or shut up, I built an architectural office for myself using the pebbled courtyard idea.

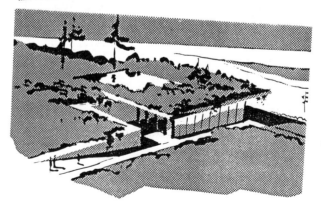

Almost all of this page is dedicated to a young architect named David Marley who was, before too long, formally join this doomly band of pilgrims 2 as it waddles down the corridors of time, spreading goodwill and truth along the way.

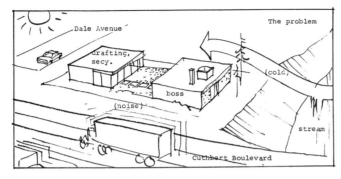

Dale Avenue

The problem

drafting, secy.

(cold)

boss

(noise)

stream

Cuthbert Boulevard

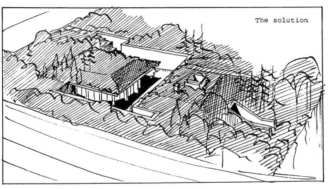

The solution

There was a tiny lot (60'x90') behind my old — dare I say it? — above-ground office in Cherry Hill, New Jersey. Used by the state highway department as a storage yard for various paving materials, it had very little going for it. On one side was a 6-lane freeway; on another a badly-polluted stream.

A conventional building — or pair of buildings — out there would have been all too appropriate in that part of New Jersey. Who would have complained about two more ugly boxes along that noisy highway? But I couldn't bear the thought, so down we went.

That's when the surprises began. The first one was that the open courtyard was actually quiet in spite of the truck traffic only 20 feet away. Another was the absolute silence of the innermost rooms. Another: discovering that some of the small animals — turtles, rabbits, moles, and mice — that moved back onto the newly green site couldn't avoid falling from the tops of the 7-foot walls, sometimes to their death.

Jessica, my number one granddaughter: how much of a page shall I dedicate to you? Would you like a bit of a chunk, a hunk, or a lot? It's up to you. I hope you pick the latter because I think you're going to do great things with your life.

Another surprise was the discovery that earth alone is not an adequate insulation material. Cold weather made _ice_ form — indoors — on surfaces nearest the out-of-doors!

And I didn't know enough to take advantage of the sun's warmth. If I'd opened the building to the south (↓) and insulated it properly it would have heated itself most of the time. Even as it was, however, the building used less heating fuel than a comparable, well-insulated above-ground office building of the same size.

The building not only attracted wildlife, it attracted tourists, publishers, reporters, architects, TV crews, relatives, and just plain well-wishers. As oil prices soared, interest in the little building soared with them, but seldom for the right reasons.

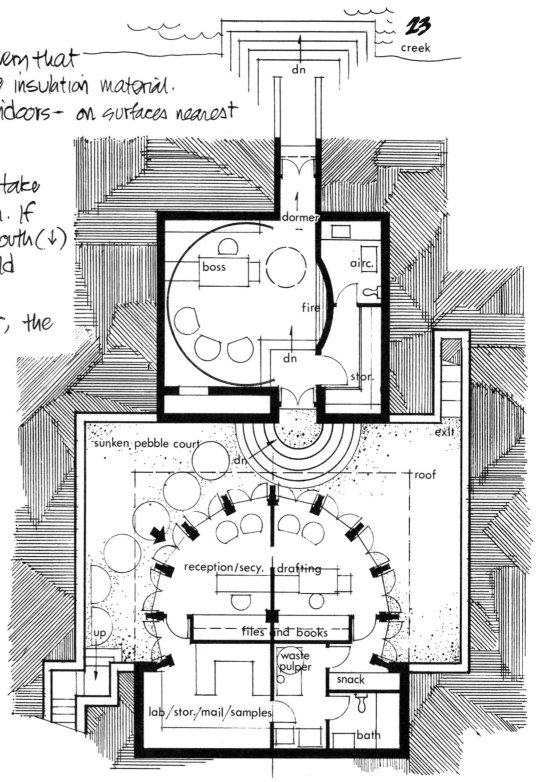

creek

dn

dormer

boss

airc.

fire

dn

stor.

exit

sunken pebble court

dn

roof

reception/secy.   drafting

up

files and books

waste pulper

snack

lab/stor./mail/samples

bath

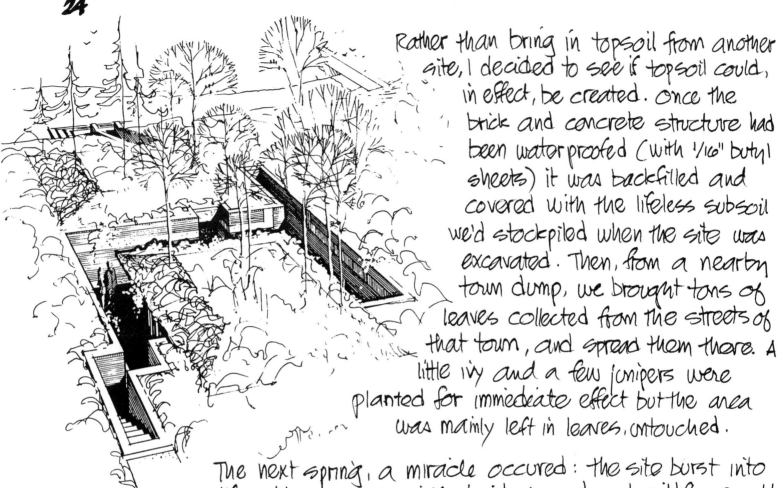

Rather than bring in topsoil from another site, I decided to see if topsoil could, in effect, be created. Once the brick and concrete structure had been waterproofed (with 1/16" butyl sheets) it was backfilled and covered with the lifeless subsoil we'd stockpiled when the site was excavated. Then, from a nearby town dump, we brought tons of leaves collected from the streets of that town, and spread them there. A little ivy and a few junipers were planted for immediate effect but the area was mainly left in leaves, untouched.

The next spring, a miracle occured: the site burst into life with every imaginable kind of weed and wildflower. It was an instant green area — without poisons, fertilizers, or topsoil. I was amazed at the variety of seeds that had stowed away on board those suburban leaves.

Within just a few years I had a jungle on my hands. If ever there was a happy site in New Jersey, this one seemed to be it. At times the bird-

I have exactly the same kind of expectations for Kate. She's following a-long a couple of years be-hind Jessica, and already I can see her special qual-ities. May I dedicate every-thing but the toxic mat-erials in this page to you, Kate Wells?

song seemed louder than the truck traffic. Maybe it was the site's way of expressing gratitude for having been spared the fate of every other site in the area. Others, if they weren't asphalted to death, were kept in a perpetual stupor with poisons, and with mowing.

Now almost 20 years have passed since the little office was built. Now that I live in Massachusetts I don't get back there very often. Who knows? Maybe there's a fast-food joint on the site today. Two or three years ago, when I was last there, I couldn't see a sign of the building from its driveway. There was just the old walkway, disappearing into a young forest.

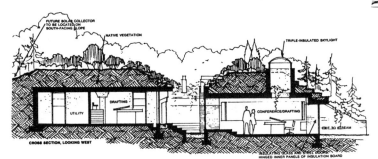

section facing west

Section facing east
The percolation bed at right
is in the center
of the driveway loop.

Come on in and join us, Samuel Apple Axle Nott. You can't escape the inevitable. A leaden chunk of this very page is set aside in your name. Who knows? Maybe you will someday catch, in the wire of the architectural undertaking, a great grotticus.

somewhere along the way, I added that "future solar collector" note (above) in an attempt to cover my failure to add the real thing.

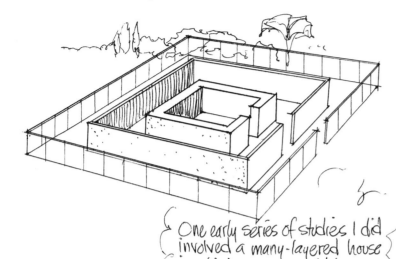

One early series of studies I did involved a many-layered house in which rooms would be peeled off, or put on, by moving in or out, depending on the degree of privacy, insulation, etc. required.

Energy conservation! It was such a hot subject in the early seventies we were all looking for ways to use less fuel. Automobiles were getting smaller, everyone was weatherstripping, and solar heating was no longer a fringe idea for use only by fanatics. Even the politicians were getting involved, offering tax credits for various conservation measures.

A dream of mine was - and still is - to build a box about the size of a large coffin, arrange it in such a way that insulation of various types and thicknesses can be applied to, and removed from, its 6 surfaces, and then crawl in and close the door (on a bitter cold winter night) and see how much insulation was needed to keep me warm, while lying in there, naked, using nothing but my body heat as the energy source. I'm still going to do it. Someday.

The sloped chamber does a lot of good things but it requires a hillside, and isn't very cheap to build even then. Clients would have to be sort of mole-like, too.

WARM AIR

COOL AIR

The sketches on these 2 pages were part of a letter I wrote as an accompaniment to the design on the next two pages. It was an idea for an energy-conserving earth-covered house to be built for a client living in North Carolina. As you'll see, it would have cost him a lot of money. He moved to another part of the country before he had a chance to find out.

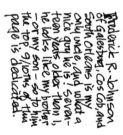

Another was the idea of lugging all your architecture around with you, but I can think of a few objections to this one, too.

It seems likely that at some time in the future, perhaps within a generation, we will learn how to heat our bodies (and other frost-vulnerable creatures and things in our buildings) without heating the buildings as well. It would save immense amounts of fuel. The practice of lighting only the surface at hand (instead of lighting an entire room) is called task lighting. Perhaps the practice of heating only bodies and other things requiring heating should be called task heating.

Heated clothing has been proposed, as has heated furniture, but it is obvious that the ideal would be the direct heating of the body. We already have such systems built into our bodies but as we become less and less active we require some sort of supplementary system. There are few highs equal to that of being made warm, in cold weather, through vigorous exercise. Maybe task heating will offer similar rewards.

Frederick R. Johnson of Galesburg, Cos Cob, and South Orleans is my only uncle. And what a nice guy he is! Seventeen years older than I, he looks like my brother — or my son — so to him the top 9/10ths of this page is dedicated.

Surely I didn't mean to propose that there be hundreds of square feet of lifeless pebbles around the house. Maybe the jiggling lines were meant to suggest mulch, or some sort of ground cover.

In any case, you've got to admit that winter nights could be mighty snug and quiet up there in those rooms above the main floor, with nothing but the sound of the wind generator to break the silence.

I never did a floor plan, apparently. These drawings were sent off to the client, getting an enthusiastic reply, but then, as I said, the job was left to die... (just as the unwary visitor might have done had she come a-running in along the entrance walk, at left, smack into the glass wall!)

LOOKS LIKE HOME ON THE RANGE OR SOMETHING, DOESN'T IT?

A wintertime cross section and a summertime cross section...

This was in 1972, long before I'd heard about the value of pulling heated air down from the top of a building (p. 81) before it can escape through the roof.

Might have been a tad cold and damp, down there on that lowest floor during the winter, even in the sunny paradise of the Carolinas.

ALTITUDE OF MIDWINTER SUN AT NOON: 26° 30'

DOUBLE INSULATED ROOF HATCH OR SKYLIGHT.

WIND-DRIVEN ELECTRIC POWER GENERATOR

NORTH SIDE EVERGREEN HEDGEROW DEFLECTS MOST COLD WINDS.

WARMEST AIR COLLECTS HERE

CLEAR STORM-PANELS ABOVE NORTHSIDE GARDENS DEFLECT COLD WINDS

EARTH    WARM BATHS    EARTH

SILENT HIDEAWAY

⇐ SOUTH    RAINWATER    NORTH ⇒

INTERIOR PERIMETER GARDENS SUPPLY FRESH FOOD AND AIR-MOISTURE. COMPOSTED ORGANIC WASTES FROM HOUSEHOLD USED AS SOIL NUTRIENTS.

SUNLIGHT PENETRATES DEEP INTO HOUSE.

WINTERTIME SLEEPING ON BALC. LEVEL?

ALTITUDE OF MIDSUMMER SUN AT NOON: 73° 30'

WIND-DRIVEN GENERATOR PROVIDES MINIMUM POWER

CHIMNEY EFFECT CREATES NATURAL DRAFT.

DECIDUOUS TREES AUTOMATICALLY BAR SUMMER SUN.

AIR-CONDIT'D. ROOM.

CROSS VENTILATION

SHADY GARDEN

⇐ SOUTH    RAINWATER RUNOFF FROM ROOF SOAKS INTO LAND    COOL AIR LIES TRAPPED IN LOW AREAS (SUMMERTIME SLEEPING?)    NORTH ⇒

Outside the family, now, the dedication go to heroes and friends. In the hero department, my first nominee is Ralph Nader, and to him I dedicate everything on this page except for two commas and part of the page no.

One of the hot-growth areas in the New Jersey suburbs of Philadelphia — Evesham Township, I think it was — was said to be considering building an addition to its municipal building. The year: 1974. "May I submit a proposal?", I asked. "Of course," came the response, so I dreamed this dream, watercolored it until it resembled an earthly paradise, and sent it in, never to be heard from again. I never saw what they built instead. I couldn't bear to. But I've seen that township. From the quaint farmlands of the sixties it has become wall-to-wall houses and shopping centers, a town without a center, without any kind of relief from the dizzying mazes of streets that seem to go nowhere.

Sour grapes.

Very sour.

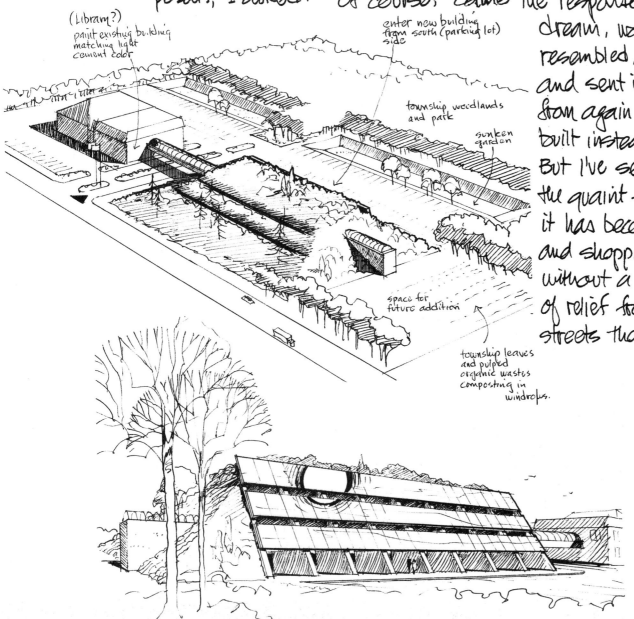

(Library?)
paint existing building matching light cement color

enter new building from south (parking lot) side

township woodlands and park

sunken garden

space for future addition

township leaves and pulped organic wastes composting in windrows.

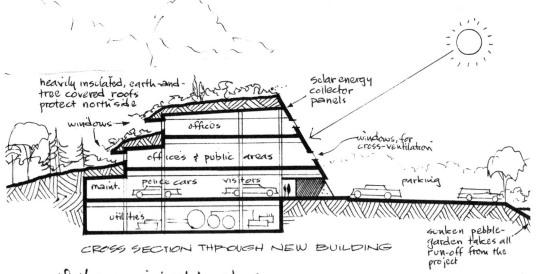

heavily insulated, earth-and-tree covered roofs protect north side

windows→

solar energy collector panels

offices

offices & public areas

windows, for cross-ventilation

maint.   police cars   visitors

parking

utilities

sunken pebble-garden takes all run-off from the project

CROSS SECTION THROUGH NEW BUILDING

If the municipal building were to be built today it would more than likely have large areas of sun-shaded glass on the south side, picking up direct (passive) solar energy rather than have the huge collector panels that were so hot for a decade.

When solar electric panels get to be cheap enough, the buildings may look like these ones again.

Unshaded south-facing walls of glass can be murderously hot in the summertime. Sun-louvers or shade trees are needed to shade the glass from the direct rays of the August sun.

DESIGN FOR A COUNTY CHILDREN'S HOME

Craig Waters, I think his name was; what a nice young man. He thought of having a legitimate theatre in the land of the philistines: the endless, look-alike New Jersey suburbs of Philadelphia.

His idea was to build at the local shopping center, making the paving do double duty in this way. He was able to get pledges for quite a lot of money but not enough to justify starting a project of this size, so the momentum was lost and — well, you know the story by now.

The fact that my daughter, Kappy, is a sculptor may have had something to do with the idea of using

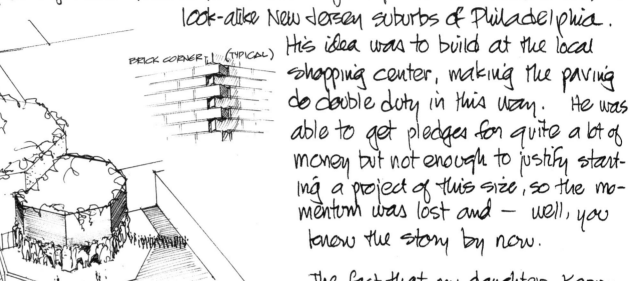

BRICK CORNER (TYPICAL)

AERIAL PERSPECTIVE SHOWING GENERAL LAYOUT, ROOFTOP PLANTINGS, AND HIDDEN AIR CONDITIONERS. NOTE SCALE OF HUMAN FIGURES WAITING IN LINE.

BELOW: PERSPECTIVE FROM PARKING LOT SHOWING 10' HIGH SCULPTURED FIGURES AROUND ENTRY PORTICO.

Then we have J. Baldwin, my longtime friend, pen-pal, Utah guide, and all-around genius and editor. This dedication plaque will make known to all who pass that to J. I dedicate 13+31/49ths of this fascinating page.

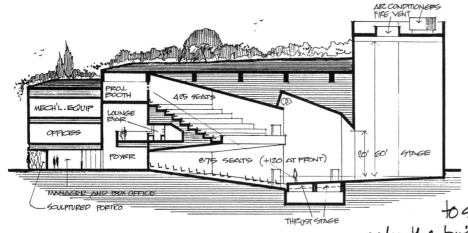

MECH'L. EQUIP
OFFICES
LOUNGE BAR
PROJ. BOOTH
425 SEATS
FOYER
875 SEATS (+120 AT FRONT)
MANAGER AND BOX OFFICE
SCULPTURED PORTICO
AIR CONDITIONERS FIRE VENT
20' 60' STAGE
THRUST STAGE

giant figures from the world of drama to support the wall.

This is, of course, stretching the idea of earth-cover a bit far... all that money to support a rooftop garden that only the birds would see — and use.

On the other hand, however, the cost of the added structure needed to carry those earth loads, when compared with the over-all cost of the project, would be almost negligible.

Ah, it would have been a dramatic building, a garden spot in a dreary shopping center.

At least it provided some happy imaginings... and more badly-needed drawing practice.

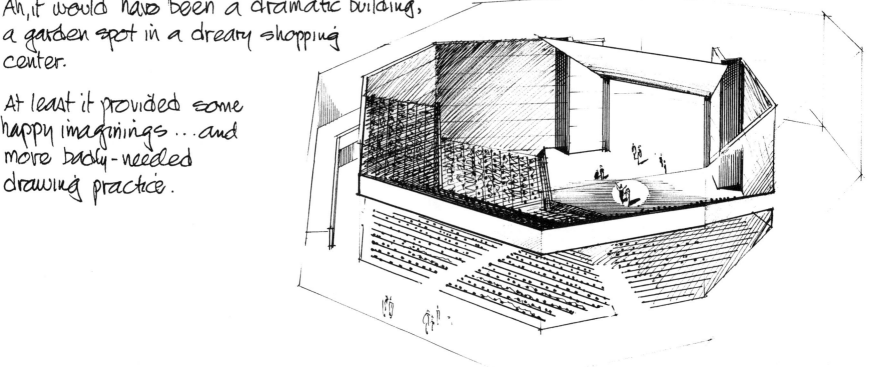

Throw away all the other pages if you must but save these two.
I want to be able to say I told you so, along about the year 2090.
Here's why: we, and all our buildings and other civilized trappings, get uprooted, moved, re-rooted, and then uprooted again, ad infinitum, or so it seems. Mobility and restlessness are our middle names. But every time we change our minds the natural world takes it on the chin. You can't clear a forest one day and replace it the next. The same is true of entire ecosystems and habitats. The cycles of change in Nature are too slow to keep pace with our restlessness.

One response would be to take away our wheels, nail us down, make us get back into the rhythms of the earth, but it's not in our nature to live that way, not any more. We're on a quest (some call it a rampage), for what, no one is sure. It seems to be leading us far out into space, far down into the heart of matter, far out to the limits of things. That's the human condition.

So rather than resist what is obviously the destiny of our race, why not accommodate it, and the natural world as well, by creating totally

Dave Deppen is the Bay Area architect who, when we were in New Jersey showed me how to design a book for self-publication. Now I must swing it without him. To you, Dave: everything on this page but the bruising off the edge.

changeable environments
within permanently immovable
earth structures?

Giant earth shelves,
built to last for
milennia, would allow
the wounds caused by their
construction time to heal, and to let the natural succession of
plants occur. Year after year, the soil would grow richer, the
wildlife more varied and abundant,
the land ever more beautiful. And,
year after year, the restless ones
would be free to move, to change
their habits, to recycle the old units,
and to live without the guilt that now
spoils our enjoyment of the world
around us, knowing as we do, that all
the best parts are soon to disappear.

We could, of course, destroy the entire
planet and move on, to another one. We
could also destroy the planet and stay
here in the ashes. Or we could stand back
and give the poor old girl another chance.

Dave Deppen, who edited Underground
Designs, p.191, used this drawing →
on its title page. Hello, Dave.

Crystals of various geometries grow uninvited in the heads of architects. One month, I find myself doing rectangles, the next: circles, followed by hexagons or free-forms. What we see here are products of mixed crystals, no doubt: squares masquerading as triangles. No matter how they actually work, thought-crystals are unending delights to their hosts. I never know, when a design starts to appear, where it comes from, or where it's going, just as I have no idea what words will appear to fill the rest of this page, still blank from here on down.

Can you imagine the kinds of fencing that would have been required to keep all those crowds of New York kids from climbing up over this little exhibit? Jim Oliver, the Aquarium director, was terribly concerned about the destruction of Jamaica Bay, hemmed in as it was, and is, by JFK airport and every other kind of urban development. He wanted to have something, even a little exhibit, to show aquarium visitors the kinds of treasures being crushed out of existence by all the mindless growth and its attendant noise and pollution.

But the funds never materialized.

exit area displays
Jamaica Bay shore birds exhibit
sand, banked against walls
exitway plank bridge over pond
44 feet square
staff work area
small exhibit tanks
demonstration area seats 30 (sunken)
entrance exhibits
wildfowl pond
pond
rail

JAMAICA BAY EXHIBIT    NEW YORK AQUARIUM    CONEY ISLAND, BROOKLYN, N. Y.    MALCOLM B. WELLS, ARCHITECT

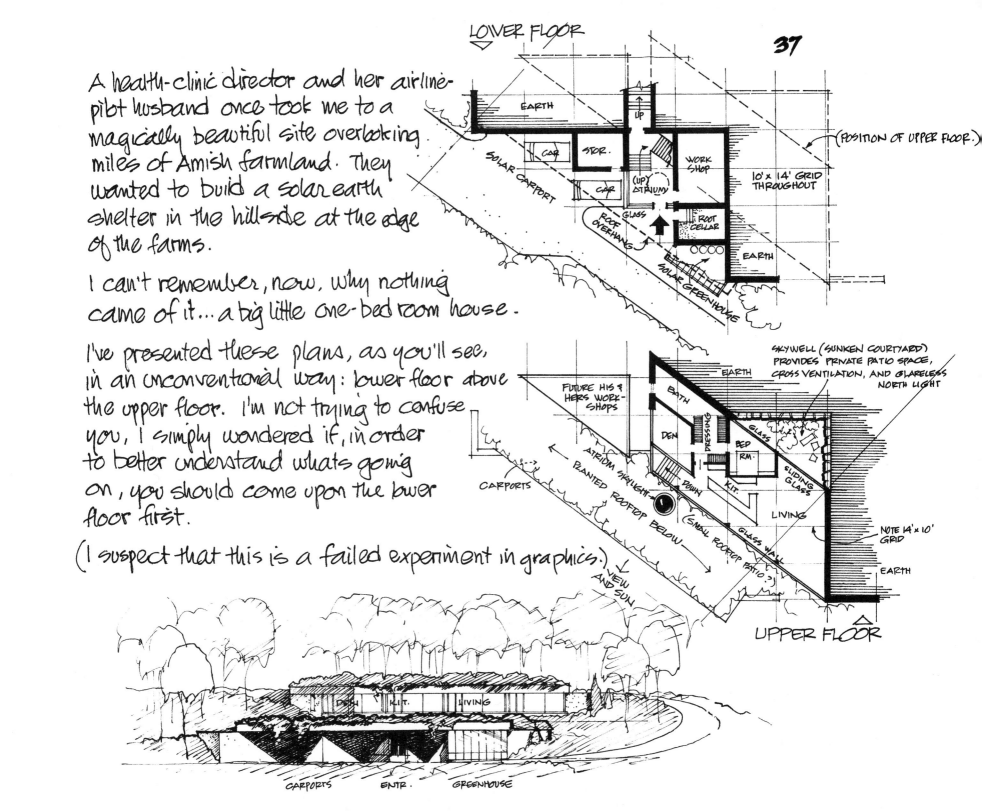

A health-clinic director and her airline-pilot husband once took me to a magically beautiful site overlooking miles of Amish farmland. They wanted to build a solar earth shelter in the hillside at the edge of the farms.

I can't remember, now, why nothing came of it... a big little one-bedroom house.

I've presented these plans, as you'll see, in an unconventional way: lower floor above the upper floor. I'm not trying to confuse you, I simply wondered if, in order to better understand what's going on, you should come upon the lower floor first.

(I suspect that this is a failed experiment in graphics.)

EARTH

SOLAR CARPORT

CAR

CAR

STOR.

UP

(UP) ATRIUM

WORK SHOP

ROOF OVERHANG

GLASS

ROOT CELLAR

SOLAR GREENHOUSE

EARTH

(POSITION OF UPPER FLOOR.)

10' x 14' GRID THROUGHOUT

FUTURE HIS & HERS WORK-SHOPS

EARTH

BATH

DEN

DRESSING

GLASS

BED RM.

SKYWELL (SUNKEN COURTYARD) PROVIDES PRIVATE PATIO SPACE, CROSS VENTILATION, AND GLARELESS NORTH LIGHT

SLIDING GLASS

CARPORTS

ATRIUM SKYLIGHT

PLANTED ROOFTOP BELOW

DOWN

KIT.

(SMALL ROOFTOP PATIO?)

LIVING

GLASS WALL

NOTE 14' x 10' GRID

EARTH

VIEW AND SUN

UPPER FLOOR

CARPORTS    ENTR.    GREENHOUSE

Now. what is all this about? These sketches turned up somewhere in my files and I decided to include them. But why? this first one relates, somehow, to the stepped-up rooms on page 26. The highest room would certainly be the warmest but unless its excess heat could be pulled down and stored in and around the lowest room, the warmth would find its way out through the upper-floor walls and windows. Has anyone built a series of rooms like this as a thermal experiment*?

This next one has an upper room, too, but I doubt if it was done for thermal reasons. Looks like a good spot for a secret pagan ritual... sunlight illuminating the altar at certain seasons... It doesn't matter; the point is that the building could be a beauty.

There simply isn't anything like earth cover to endow a building with a sense of eternal appropriateness.

Take a look out columns. Can you here between these massive see, out there in the distance, the bands of windows that identify the far-away hills as human habitations?...terrace after green terrace, down the slopes, housing thousands of people without displacing the plants and animals entitled to share the land with their human kin.

Paul Giambarba came to see me on business 10 years ago and we've been friends ever since. But he and Pam have moved to California! What kind of friends are they? Good ones, I say, and to them I dedicate a huge portion of this very page.

* "Yes," said my friends at Raven Rocks,
"remember the Karen Terry House?"
(The Passive Solar Energy Book. Mazria. PP 42-43.)

Not many little furry creatures live here. A few mice, perhaps, and Velda in her new mink coat. The average underground house in America is an architectural horror — the worst of suburban consumerist values under the worst of suburban landscapes: the toxic green* lawn. Energy is conserved here, all right, but strictly for the wrong reasons. They use the savings to buy more gadgets. First it was the CB radio, then the video games, the computer, the VCR, and the compact disc. Now it's the ever-helpful fax, linking them to all the other people who share their tastes and values.

Here's a more altruistic family. They saved their money in the hope of saving the land but when that pile of dirt hits the roof...crash! The land will land in the living room. You have to be careful when you place earth on a roof, even a carefully-designed one (and that's the only kind to have).

Construction loads are far more severe, sometimes, than the long-term ones.

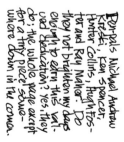

Pen-pals Michael Andrew Kresei, Ken Spencer, Hunter Collins, Hughtos-to and Ray Mahar. Do they not brighten my days enough to earn this virtual dedication? Yes, they do; the whole page except for a tiny piece some-where down in the corner.

*Thanks to Milwaukee naturalist Lorrie Otto for the "toxic green" label.

In the early seventies, the British government was said to have been offering financial aid to developers willing to invest in its Turks & Caicos Islands, down there below the Bahamas, so some rather naively idealistic investors flew me down to those gorgeous and, at that time, largely unspoiled islands

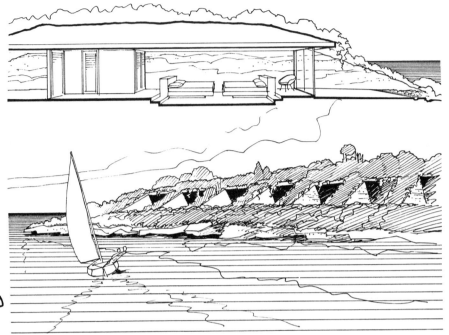

to see if simple, environmentally-benign projects would be encouraged. The answer from the authorities there being a qualified yes, I returned to New Jersey and worked out this carved-into-the-coral-rock design.

In the Turks and Caicos Islands, everything was scarce. Fresh water, wood, cement... even skilled labor... but the people of the area were extremely friendly, enthusiastic, and willing. All that was

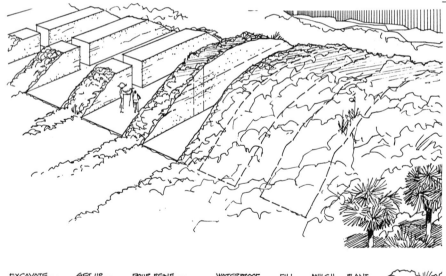

EXCAVATE...
SOFT ROCK

SET UP...
FORMS

POUR REINF...
CONCR. SLAB

WATERPROOF...
SLAB

FILL ....MULCH....PLANT

needed was a nod from the Crown. That nod, apparently, was a bit more difficult to get than was at first indicated. As the red tape piled up, the investors began to lose interest, and, before long, this dream, called Stone Angel Harbor (or perhaps Harbour, down there) evaporated, as had so many of the others.

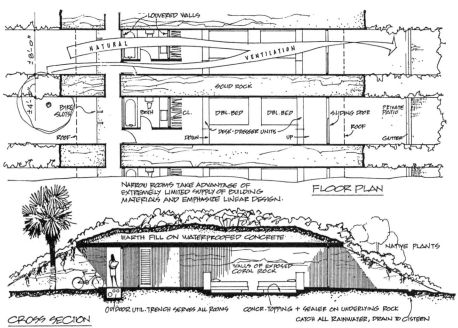

LOUVERED WALLS

NATURAL VENTILATION

SOLID ROCK

BIKE SLOTS

BATH · CL. · DBL. BED · DBL. BED · SLIDING DOOR · PRIVATE PATIO

DESK-DRESSER UNITS

DOWN · UP · ROOF

ROOF · GUTTER

NARROW ROOMS TAKE ADVANTAGE OF EXTREMELY LIMITED SUPPLY OF BUILDING MATERIALS AND EMPHASIZE LINEAR DESIGN.

FLOOR PLAN

EARTH FILL ON WATERPROOFED CONCRETE

NATIVE PLANTS

WALLS OF EXPOSED CORAL ROCK

CROSS SECTION

OUTDOOR UTIL. TRENCH SERVES ALL ROOMS

CONCR. TOPPING + SEALER ON UNDERLYING ROCK CATCH ALL RAINWATER, DRAIN TO CISTERN

But what could have been simpler than carving 8-foot slots through a low ridge of coral rock? The natives had been cutting that stone for years. Add a roof slab, waterproofing, and soil, and you'd have guest rooms naturally cooled beneath the blazing tropical sun.

This idea was resurrected in a somewhat different form for the equally-ill-fated China project shown on pages 126 and 127. No doubt it will turn up again, somewhere, so be forewarned: if you come to me with a commission to design a hotel in a hilltop this is what you're likely to get.

It will, of course, be beautifully redesigned, but don't let that fool you.

I don't want to forget my favorite editors, none of whom I've met: Peter Fossel, Toni Rawls, and Chuck McCullagh. I want to make them immortal by airing their names here so I dedicate to them at least signs of even-thing visible on this page.

Every once in a while, I walk away from a client before he has a chance to walk away from me. Unless I'm mistaken, that was the case with this project for what was to have been called Ocean City Community College, in Maryland. The site was the all-too-familiar farmland about to be asphalted by suburbia, and, once I heard that the school would stress the notion of self-

reliance, I produced a whole sheaf of drawings illustrating this sort of design. It was received with enthusiasm but funds were tight and the project began to drag. At a second meeting, I decided to see what the better-known part of Ocean City, Maryland, was like. I pictured a quaint seaside village something like the Ocean City, New Jersey, of my childhood. Instead, I found a wall of high-rises running for miles along the beach. It was a carbon copy of Miami Beach's Collins Avenue.

I never bothered this client again. That tortured ocean-front had done me in.

Three writers have tried to write about this underground architect. All went numb too bored to do it. Brad Lemley was the exception. His writing is so good the subject doesn't matter, so to you, Brad, I dedicate all but 3 words printed on this page.

Cape Cod, on the other hand — back in 1974 — <u>was</u> like the New Jersey of the Thirties. I was amazed to find that the peninsula was a vast pine forest with a few small towns along one or the other of its saltwater sides. As soon as I saw it, my head packed up

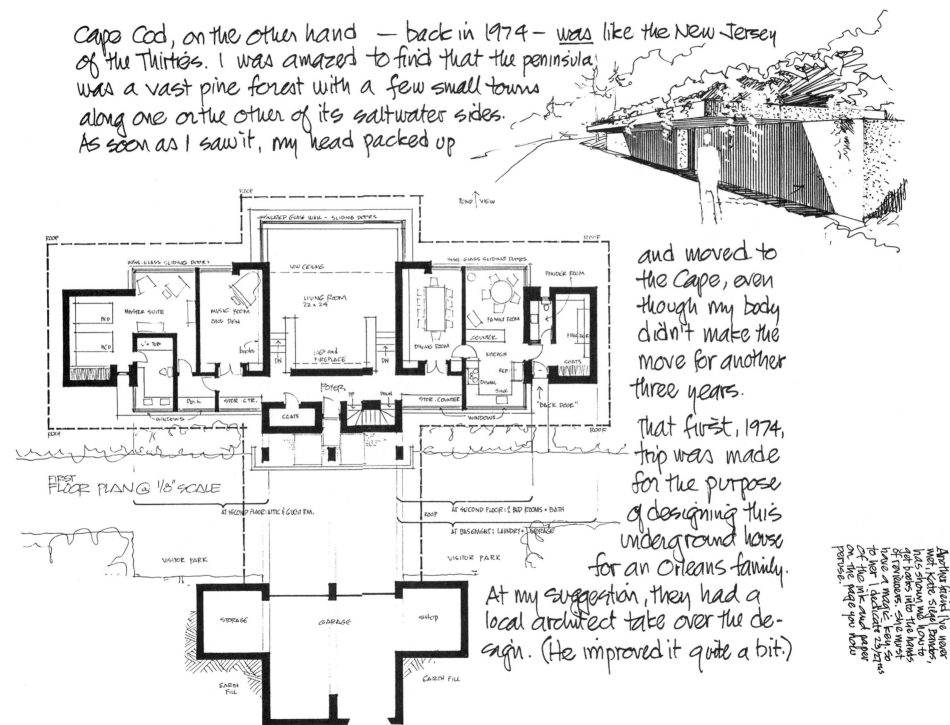

POND ↑ VIEW

ROOF

INSULATED GLASS WALL - SLIDING DOORS

ROOF

INSUL. GLASS SLIDING DOOR

LOW CEILING

INSUL. GLASS SLIDING DOORS

POWDER ROOM

BED

MASTER SUITE

MUSIC ROOM AND DEN

LIVING ROOM 22 x 24

FAMILY ROOM

FREEZER

BED

'TUB

books

1:6½ and FIREPLACE

DINING ROOM

COUNTER

COATS

DN

DN

KITCHEN

PDL

STOR. CTR.

FOYER

up

DOWN

STOR. COUNTER

REF.

DISH.

SINK

"BACK DOOR"

COATS

WINDOWS

COATS

WINDOWS

ROOF

ROOF

FIRST FLOOR PLAN @ ⅛" SCALE

AT SECOND FLOOR: ATTIC & GUEST RM.

ROOF

AT SECOND FLOOR: 2 BED ROOMS + BATH

AT BASEMENT: LAUNDRY + STORAGE

VISITOR PARK

VISITOR PARK

STORAGE

GARAGE

SHOP

EARTH FILL

EARTH FILL

and moved to the Cape, even though my body didn't make the move for another three years.

That first, 1974, trip was made for the purpose of designing this underground house for an Orleans family.

At my suggestion, they had a local architect take over the design. (He improved it quite a bit.)

Another friend I've never met, Kate Siegel Pandos, has shown me how to get books into the hands of reviewers. She must have a magic pen, so to her I dedicate 23/27ths of the ink and paper on the page you peruse.

This house was based on an idea so simple that many versions of it have been built. The original one, the one called SOLARIA, below, was built at Indian Mills, New Jersey, in 1974. My friends Bob & Nancy Homan were willing to take a chance on several then-untried systems, the main ones being solar heating and earth cover. I'd never piled dirt on a roof with such a slope but after some trial and error (I don't want to talk about it) horizontal cleats were added just under the rubber waterproofing sheet, and the earthen fill stayed right where it was put. For a solar heating system we chose the super-simple trickle-down panels invented by Dr. Harry Thomason. Both the earth cover and the solar heating worked like charms, cutting energy bills to insignificance, and that's the way it went for 10 or 12 years. Then some

There's hardly room here to dedicate most of this page to all my friends at Raven Rocks but that's still what I intend to do. To all of you Ohioans along Crum Road — and 145, who've been such good friends, 14, 17, this page is dedicated exclusively to you.

leaks began to appear. The Homans did everything to caulk and seal the openings as they were discovered but the problem kept growing. It was our first experience — and only experience, so far — in which thick, tough butyl rubber sheets admitted water.

After some awful messes and after trying everything else to solve the problem, the Homans bit the bullet and took all those tons of earth off of the roof. The butyl, they found, had been riddled by ... what? It took some time to deduce that beetle larva (that had, apparently, been in the big roof timbers from the start) had bored through insulation, plywood, rubber, and earth in order to reach the sunlight. And the Homans, having had enough of roof troubles for a while, put a conventional roof on Solaria for the time being.

The moral of the story could very well be <u>don't build underground!</u>  could be. I prefer to think that the advantages still far outweigh the disadvantages, and that we must all be prepared to accept the occasional hard knocks dealt us by fate as graciously and as good-humoredly as the Homans did.

My first underground design for them, by the way, before my solar conversion, looked like L. (——→)

You'll see more of this one on the photo pages.

The Cary Arboretum of The New York Botanical Garden is in a lovely valley at Millbrook, New York, not far from Poughkeepsie. When the trustees of the Arboretum invited me to design their new Plant Science Building they not only offered to try some new ideas, they actually insisted upon it.

The result: earth shelter, solar heating, thermal mass, exterior insulation, task lighting, summer sunshading, water-conserving plumbing fixtures, heat recovery systems, and, last but not least, appropriately, a landscape of native plants.

Unfortunately, the solar heating system turned out to be unsatisfactory and was removed, delighting some anti-solar skeptics who assumed, incorrectly, that the sun itself had somehow let us down.

Here's part of a letter I wrote to the owners of a monastery, also in New York State, who had invited me to join them for a couple of days before submitting a proposal. The robes and the meditation to which they exposed me never took root but the wholesome food and the silence, not to mention the genuine friendliness, really moved me.

The pages of design ideas I sent them seemed to move them in return. We stayed in pretty close contact for a while.

Maybe the phone will ring any day now.

Break the car-mood dramatically; abruptly; with a land-centered, rather than a man-centered, entrance to the community itself.

I see a long, gently-sloping up-ramp as the central trunk of the country center. From an entry/foyer, which might include some business offices as well as the usual shoe-removal, coat-hanging, and clothes-changing rooms under its low roof, one could pass through a series of ever-loftier, ever more awesome spaces toward the heart of the complex. The point, of course, would be to use architectural devices to put the jangling 1975 world behind, both physically and symbolically. The ceiling might start at a low seven feet, and slowly climb to greater heights as the space became narrower and narrower, the sky-glimpses fewer and fewer, until the space was nearly vertical; silent; shadowed... like this:

You might very easily create this kind of changing space-character by doing the work sequentially, in order, starting right at the entrance, using only untrained people working with the crudest of tools, and slowly letting the quality of the work improve as the workers gained experience, until, deeper inside the hill, nearer the entrances to the Zendo and the Buddha Hall, some very fine finishes might be achieved. I don't think you'd have to worry about the finishes becoming too perfect, not as long as human beings were involved.

natural cooling, and even heating, using the earth mass around a building, is an idea that continues to generate a lot of interest. I was all set to install an earth-tube temperature-moderating system at my first Cape Cod house when I heard someone say that moisture condensing in such conduits could act as a breeding ground for Legionaires' Disease. That did it: I haven't done an earth-tube system to this day, even though it is obviously no problem to provide condensate drains in the pipes.

A glance at this diagram will make it obvious that cool air would flow naturally down through the building in hot weather, and that (relatively) warm air would rise through the building in the winter. That's practically the whole story on earth tubes.

John Hait, who has developed earth covered houses that store enough summer heat to warm themselves all winter, uses earth tubes extensively, snaking them for, I believe, hundreds of feet through the soil before they enter the structures.

Laurie Virr was still a student when he came to work for me in 1963. Now he's a gifted architect in Australia. To him and to his wife, Mary, my old friends, I dedicate quite a bit of this page. It's another example of my generous nature, I suppose.

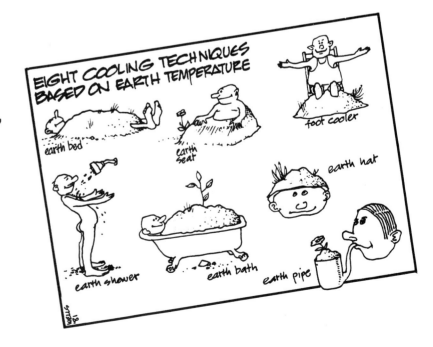

EIGHT COOLING TECHNIQUES BASED ON EARTH TEMPERATURE

earth bed

earth seat

foot cooler

earth shower

earth bath

earth hat

earth pipe

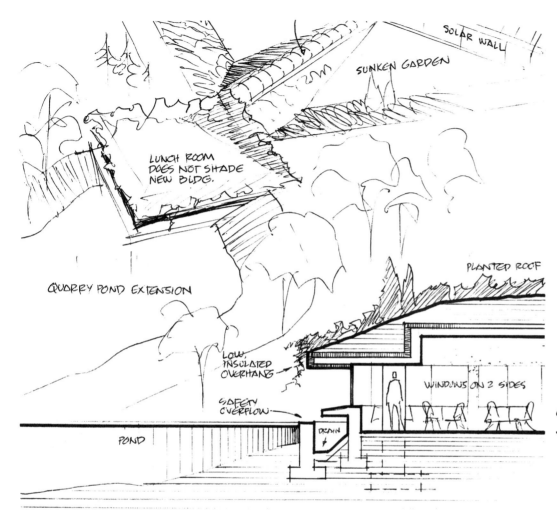

SOLAR WALL

SUNKEN GARDEN

LUNCH ROOM DOES NOT SHADE NEW BLDG.

QUARRY POND EXTENSION

LOW, INSULATED OVERHANG

PLANTED ROOF

SAFETY OVERFLOW

WINDOWS ON 2 SIDES

POND

DRAIN

POND COULD BE MADE TO COME ALMOST UP TO WINDOW SILL (TABLE TOP) LEVEL.

You'll see this idea over and over again in these pages (pp. 104, 105; 140, 141) because I know it can be dramatic and trouble-free. A pond, either natural or artificial, is made to come right up to your window-sill, causing perhaps some initial uneasiness but after that, I think, endless fascination as ducks, geese, and sea monsters swim to within a few feet of you. This first attempt to sell the idea was made to a publisher in Pennsylvania who wanted to build an employees' (organic food, no less) cafeteria near a little pond on his property. I simply wanted to extend the pond a bit. If I were to do the pond-sill now I'd slope the top of the dam wall so that ice expansion would ride up and over the top instead of toppling the wall.

And what about new friends? What about Stephanie and Frank Foster? Even though both of them shot me I lived to tell the story. This is your page—most of it is S. and F. Do with it what you will. This will probably make you famous.

During a telephone call from one of the more rapacious land
developers in New Jersey, I found myself doing this doodle
of architecture,
greed, cruelty
and sins of all kinds.
This was in the mid-seventies,
sometime.

I'd been ashamed and embarrassed for years
by what I and all my fellow architects had done to the
American land but I don't think I'd thought about the true extent

Marie and John Schwalbe
live in the very heart of
bustling downtown Brewster.
How can they stand that
hectic life? I don't know
but I want to dedicate 2/5
of a page to John, and
21/50ths to Marie. Good
people, good friends.

of our roles in the scandal until I stopped to examine my telephone doodle. It had been aimed at the developer to whom I was speaking but it was obviously a picture of me. With my license from the state, with my pencil and a t-square, I'd be happy to "improve" any site for you if you'd just pay me a fee. Maybe I don't do ticky-tacky boxes but my work is still so far from the ideal I might as well be doing them.

the Architect

This cartoon, which grew out of the doodle at left, turned up in many places, surprising me in my travels to architectural schools.

All but 3/100th of this page is dedicated to that very special person who, in my absent-minded-ness, I've failed to mention, even though you mean so much to me. This special catch-all dedication is for you.

Among the titles I've considered using on my underground books have been

**IT'S ALL MY VAULT,**

**BEST CELLAR,**

and this one, ———→ seen here as part of a proposal I once sent to a publisher.

I want very badly to do a house that looks for all the world like a hill, and I want to build it so that all the floors, both indoors and out, are indeed on the level.

UNDERGROUND DESIGNS FOR THE 1990s & BEYOND

11"

8½"

**ON THE LEVEL**

by MALCOLM WELLS

The title will have 4 levels of meaning:
1) Straight talk about the pros and cons of earth shelter,
2) Putting to rest the fear that you must go down into an underground building,
3) Full access by the handicapped, and
4) The potential for using storage carts (holding everything from cleaning equipment and home repair tools to little-used cook-ware and out-of-season clothes), making every part of the house easily reached and served. Tax records, party games... a category for each cart.

Ronald North died in a Marine helicopter accident in 1989. Too young. He was my nephew. I should dedicate an extra page or two to him but I know he would want more than his share. So Ron, you get .91 of a page as my memorial to you.

The floors will of course be pitched as much as is required for proper drainage, and to allow for future settlement of the soil, but to anyone visiting them they will be essentially flat. Toddlers can toddle, oldsters can waddle, and all the wheeled devices in our lives will roll through the spaces with ease where in most buildings steps and curbs and too-narrow doors have even the strongest of us groaning as we carry big bundles, 5-gallon paint buckets, pianos, refrigerators, and 155-mm howitzers from room to room.

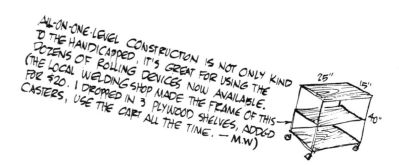

ALL-ON-ONE-LEVEL CONSTRUCTION IS NOT ONLY KIND TO THE HANDICAPPED, IT'S GREAT FOR USING THE DOZENS OF ROLLING DEVICES NOW AVAILABLE. (THE LOCAL WELDING SHOP MADE THE FRAME OF THIS FOR $20. I DROPPED IN 3 PLYWOOD SHELVES, ADDED CASTERS, USE THE CART ALL THE TIME. —M.W)

25"  15"  40"

"You want <u>on the level</u>," said fate. "Here, I'll give you on the level. How's this?"

Someone in Ft. Worth with a lot of land had been moved by pictures of my work and, as a result, invited me to design a house out there — <u>way out</u> there. In true western-hospitality style I was sent first-class plane fare, visitor information books,     and a hotel reservation!

To all my brothers- and sisters-in-law greetings. Most of what you see on this entire page is dedicated entirely to you. It will bring you fame and happiness beyond your wildest dreams so get ready to stand in the spotlight.

It was the royal treatment and I lapped it up.

I was met at the airport, wined, dined, and taken to my hotel. In my room I found rented-car keys, a map of the route to the site, anti-chigger lotion, and a snake-bite kit! And when I got to the site, there, believe it or not, was a picnic lunch in a cooler/hamper, waiting for me at the gate.

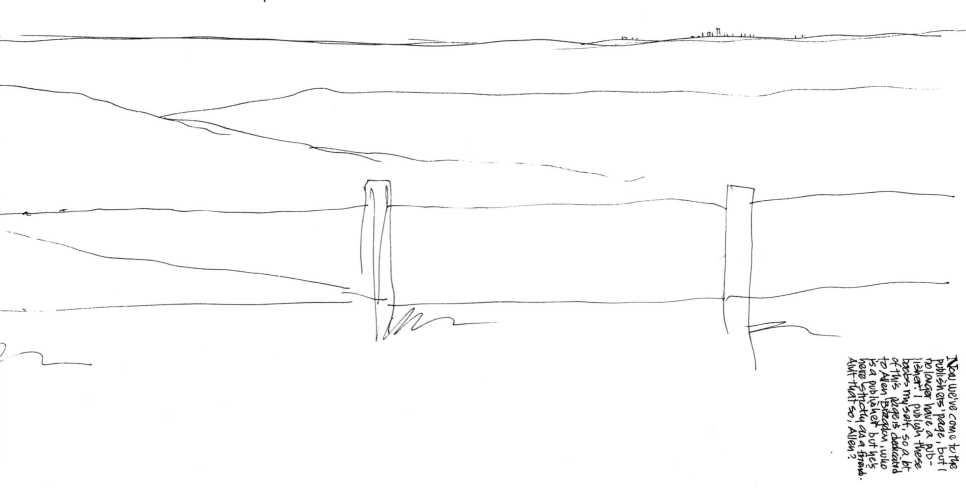

Now we've come to the publishers page, but I no longer have a publisher! I publish these books myself, so a bit of this page is dedicated to Allen Brazen, who is a publisher but he's here strictly as a friend. Aint that so, Allen?

The owners were, among their many other interests, avid vegetable gardeners. They wanted what might be called a gentleman's farm, out there on the plains. They saw their land as a Ft. Worth suburb and, indeed, I could see the towers of the city on the horizon when I visited their land (keeping one eye out for the rattlers I knew were behind every blade of grass). The owners wanted to divide their holdings into a lot of mini-farms for people with similar interests, 10 or 20 acres to each site.

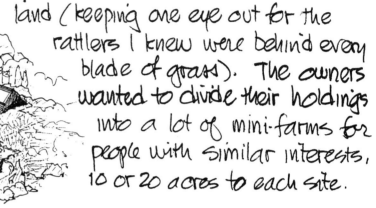

I just couldn't imagine putting their little farm complex out on the naked plain if it would make a nasty little bump on the land, so I proposed a sunken courtyard reached by driving gently down a long, curving driveway at such a gradual slope the earth banks along the way would seem to rise up out of the land until suddenly there was the courtyard, as lush and green as only that land can be when water is available. Everything was to be earth covered except for a great long living area in which a garden — with trees — and a pool would lie beneath a conventional, but skylighted roof.

Everything went along smoothly. The owners were enthusiastic. I began

With these moving words, I hereby dedicate all but three letter a's on this page to Lois & Bill Racz for being such good friends and for having such good liberal views in these strongly conservative times. Hang on to those values!

to develop details, to work out a dimensioned floor plan, to think about getting a Texas architect to tackle the job of producing construction drawings, and then...

oh, no!

...oh yes. Circumstances combined to make the move untimely for the owners, and they had to cancel the project.

That won't stop me from showing the rest of it to you, however.

And that's my Texas story.

For a final look at this house be sure to visit the next 2 pages.

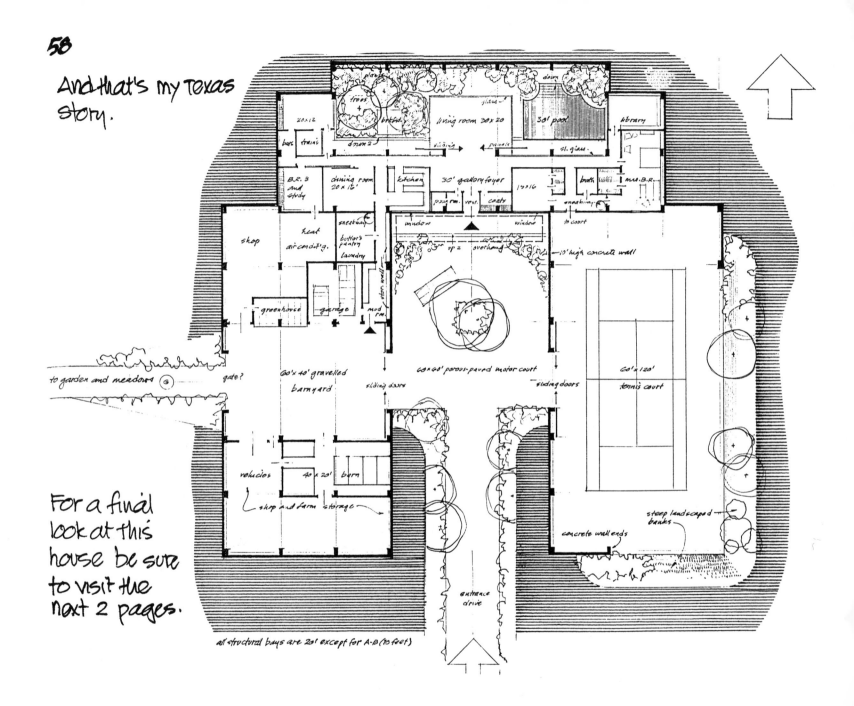

living room 30 x 20

30' pool

library

20 x 12

bar trains

dining 2

sliding

panels

st. glass

B.R. 3 and study

dining room 20 x 16'

kitchen

30' gallery foyer

17 x 16

bath

mrs. B.R.

pwr. rm. rest. coats

to court

shop

heat

air condit'g.

butler's pantry

sneakway

window

window

to court

10' high concrete wall

overhang

greenhouse

garage

mud rm.

shop and farm storage

to garden and meadows

gate?

60' x 40' gravelled barnyard

sliding doors

60' x 60' porous-paved motor court

sliding doors

60' x 120' tennis court

vehicles

40' x 20' barn

steep landscaped banks

concrete wall ends

entrance drive

all structural bays are 20' except for A-B (10 feet)

I've always wanted to bring a shingled roof right up out of the earth. Would it work? Of course it would work, easily, in a land not subject to hard freezes. The shingles, made of ceramic tile, would be set in mastic, perhaps, on the waterproofing, and then, as they came up out of the earth, they could be nailed conventionally to the roof deck.

Would the house itself have worked? Of course. The only problem I could foresee would be that of excessive humidity in the living/garden/pool area. But, with everything else behind glass partitions, the tropical climate of the great room would be no harder to manage than a room in Florida.

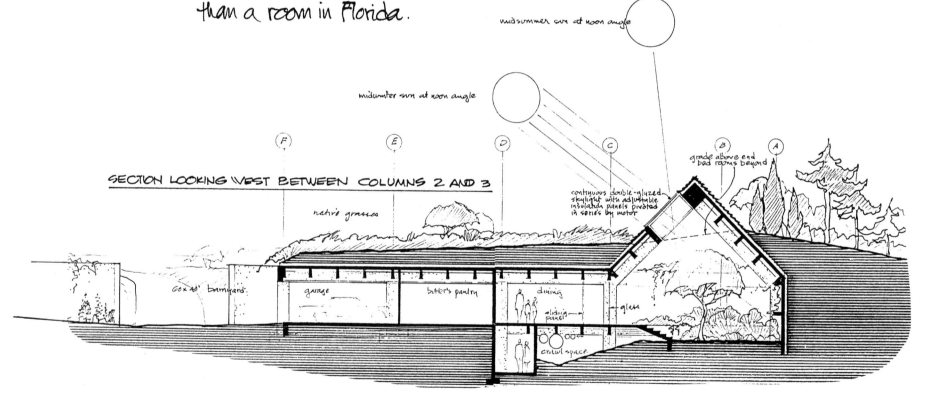

SECTION LOOKING WEST BETWEEN COLUMNS 2 AND 3

And now, if you'll forgive another abrupt change of subject, we come to the little house that, with a few modifications, can be entered from the south side as well as (as is shown here) from the north. This plan originated in 1977, and for 12 years it marinated in my head until, in 1988, it was ready to appear in POPULAR SCIENCE Magazine as the "Do It Your way Earth Shelter".

For details of that design be sure not to miss page 185. 184, too.

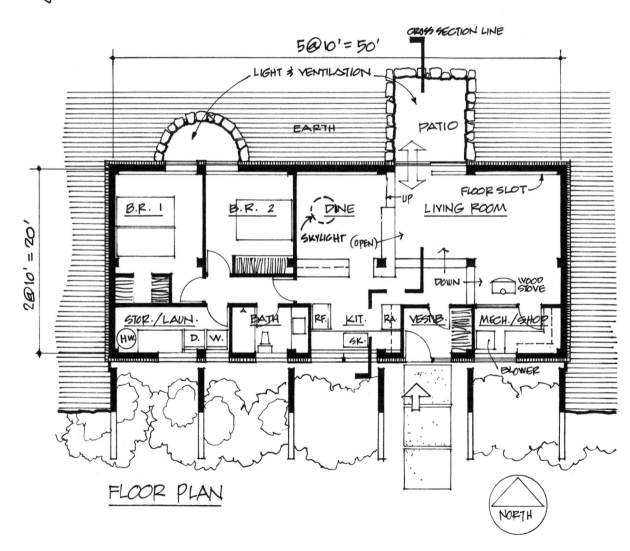

FLOOR PLAN

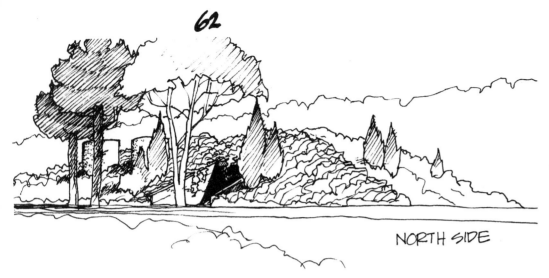

NORTH SIDE

Mid-Eighties: Still working on it. The different versions get to look so much alike it's hard to keep them straight. Is this, for instance, the north side of the north entrance version? And does it go with the drawings below? Or is north the same as south in Australia at this time of year?

Something like that.

Natural cross ventilation, daylighted both sides.

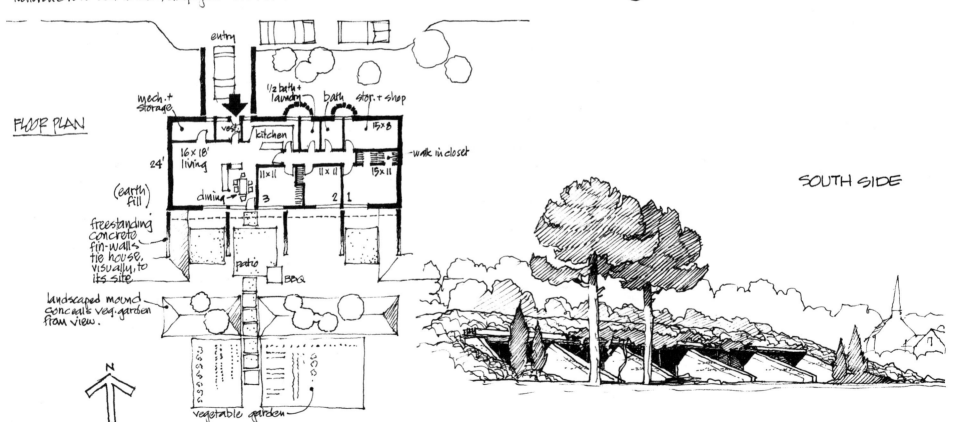

entry

mech. + storage

1/2 bath + laundry

bath

stor. + shop

FLOOR PLAN

vest.

kitchen

15 x 8

16 x 18' living

walk in closet

24'

11 x 11

11 x 11

15 x 11

(earth fill)

dining

3

2  1

freestanding concrete fin-walls tie house, visually, to its site

patio

BBQ

landscaped mound conceals veg. garden from view.

N

vegetable garden

SOUTH SIDE

Well, then this must be the south side of the south entrance house.
And this is its cross section.

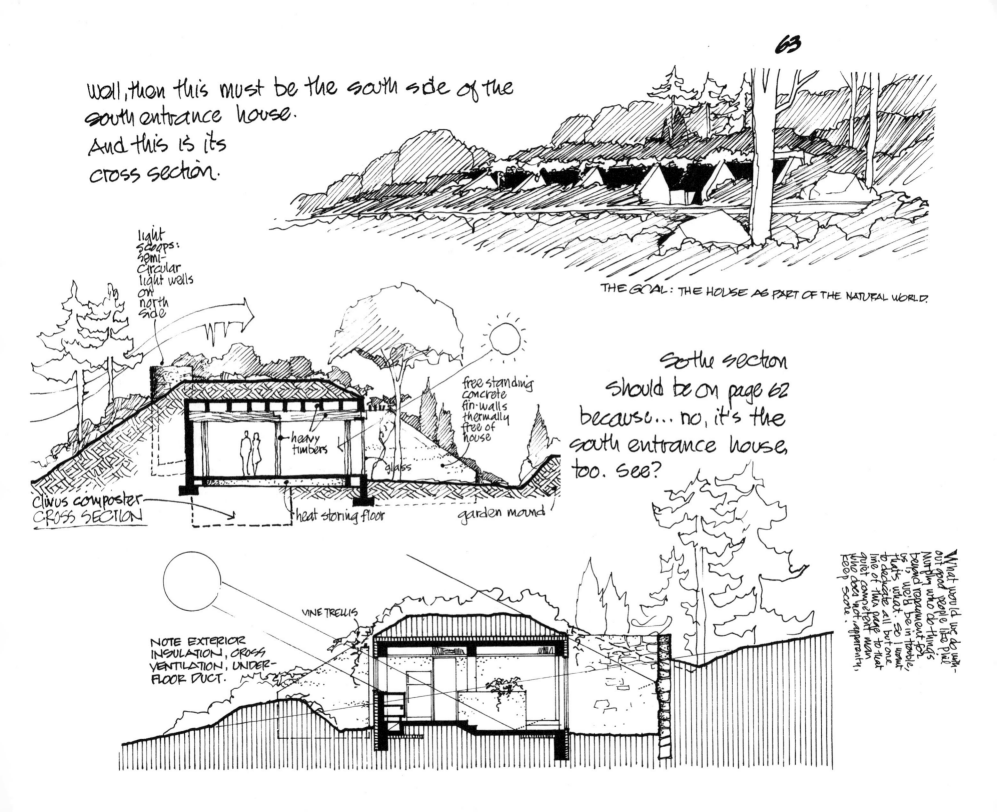

THE GOAL: THE HOUSE AS PART OF THE NATURAL WORLD.

light scoops: semi-circular light wells on north side

free standing concrete fin-walls thermally free of house

heavy timbers

glass

Clivus composter CROSS SECTION

heat storing floor

garden mound

So the section should be on page 62 because... no, it's the south entrance house, too. See?

NOTE EXTERIOR INSULATION, CROSS VENTILATION, UNDERFLOOR DUCT.

VINE TRELLIS

What would we do without good people like Phil Murphy who do things beyond repayment for us? We'd be in trouble, that's what. So I want to dedicate all but one line of this page to that quiet competent man who does not, apparently, keep score.

plenty of glass on the south side
small windows or doors on the north ...

That's what I was trying to say all along. Sun in, cold out.

The perspective above was done for some prospective clients who didn't think it possible to divide glass areas into large and small panes successfully. I won the battle but lost the war.

All the bits and pieces of pages left over from the dedication have been collected here. A special prize to be awarded to anyone who sends me ten or twenty thousand dollars in cash to help reduce the mortgage. Think about it. Everyone.

"...the earth-cast buildings
of Riviera architect Jacques Couelle..."
(see page 5.)

In 1971, The Today Show
invited me to talk about
underground buildings.
I had just four days in which to build this model, so I worked
non-stop. Rooftop wildlife ponds, organic gardens on each level,
composted wastes... it generated a flurry of letters, and then: nothing.

From "Penn's Sylvania", an article I wrote for Charrette,
the journal of the Pennsylvania Society of Architects, in 1965.

From "Nowhere to Go But Down", Progressive Architecture.
February, 1965. (see page 6.)

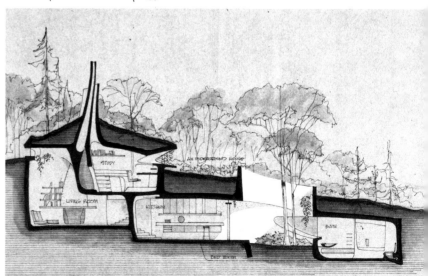

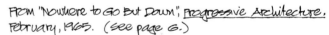

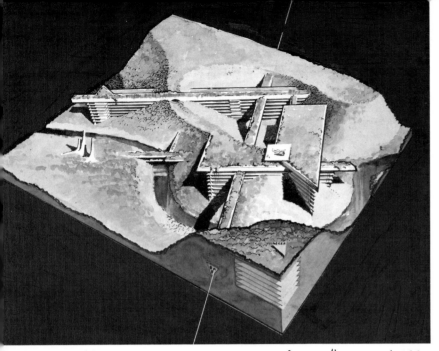

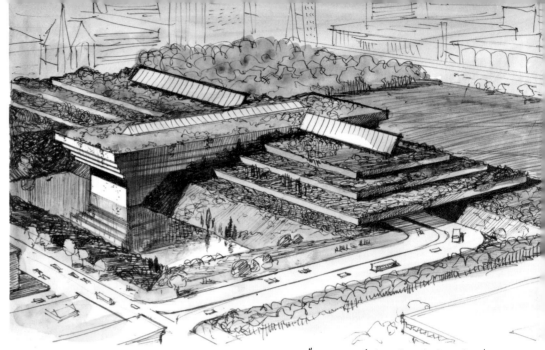

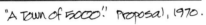
"A Town of 5000" Proposal, 1970.

1969 "Museum of The Future", done for the American Association of Museums, the design featured earth cover, solar heating, underground parking, on-site composting of organic wastes, a wildlife refuge, natural plantings, and a great percolation bed/retention basin for the site's run-off. (See page 14.)

"Low and Bermed", the little house featured in the June, 1984, issue of Popular Science. (See page 138.)

One of two designs possible with a single floor plan, this version has its main entrance on the north....

....and this, on the south. Both were published by <u>Popular Science</u> in April, 1989. (See page 184.)

1978. The newly-completed Plant Science Building of The New York Botanical Garden's Cary Arboretum at Millbrook, New York. Photo: Artog. (See page 46.)

Photo: Ken Basmajian.

Courtyard,
Cherry Hill underground
office.

My first underground building.
the office at Cherry Hill, New Jersey.
1970. (See page 22.)

(See page 22.)

Photo: Artog.

The tireless champion of all that is good, seen here upstaging his own building. House at Cape Cod. 1980. Photo: Lou Penfield. (See page 96.)

Another view of it, featuring the gifted touch of landscape designer Shirley Dorkin of Cherry Hill, N.J.

Her design touch is equally in evidence in this interior shot of the Cape Cod house. Note the low-cost, low-maintenance floor of rough concrete, stained and sealed.

1978. The original design for the Cape Cod house, it would have sacrificed view for sunlight, and I decided against it.

Locust Hill at Raven Rocks, Beallsville, Ohio.
Don't miss the story of this fascinating
project. It starts on page 82.

LOCUST HILL FROM THE SOUTHWEST
MALCOLM WELLS, ARCHITECT 8/89

A cross section
through Locust Hill, showing
all the ways in which sunlight
will penetrate deep into this
hill-sheltered structure. South is to
the left, north to the right.

If the gardens I've seen at Raven Rocks are any indication,
this one will be almost unbelievable. To me, it's as much
a part of the design as the walls and roof,
expressing as it does, so much about
life, sunlight, earth, and the
miracle of growth.

THE NORTHSIDE GARDEN AT LOCUST HILL
MALCOLM WELLS, ARCHITECT 8/89

Great care is taken
each step of the way at Locust Hill
out of respect for the materials themselves
and the jobs that will be asked of them
over the coming centuries.

The day I got to pose as a construction man, vibrating the concrete as it went into the form at Locust Hill. With me, and doing the real work, were Warren Stetzel and Tim Starbuck.

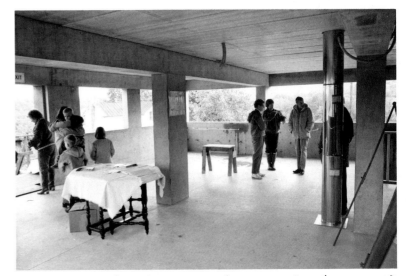

The Sidwell house at Raven Rocks. (See page 88.)

The Underground Gallery at Brewster on Cape Cod, where I sit as I write these words. The building, still incomplete, cries out for the plants that will, in time, make it look almost as good as I pictured it when I did this rendering. (see page 108.)

By now, the meaning of just about everything on this cross section is no doubt evident but it does contain one element worth mentioning: deep excavation.

The vertical shading indicates backfill. Its depth on the north side of the structure suggests the great depth of cut required for underground buildings, particularly for those built on hillsides. The related problems are 1) the possibility of cave-ins, 2) the need to remove existing vegetation far to the north

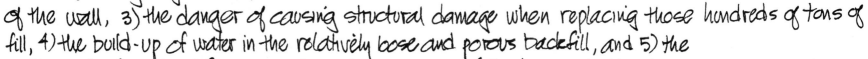

of the wall, 3) the danger of causing structural damage when replacing those hundreds of tons of fill, 4) the build-up of water in the relatively loose and porous backfill, and 5) the settlement of the backfill, even after it has been carefully tamped in thin layers.

Backfill, as it settles, or sinks, takes down with it such things as insulation board and (sometimes) waterproofing. It can also rupture buried utility lines!

The watchwords: be careful!

WE'RE LOOKING FOR A MORE NATURAL, MORE APPROPRIATE ARCHITECTURE, AN ARCHITECTURE THAT LOOKED AS IF IT HAD GROWN THERE ...

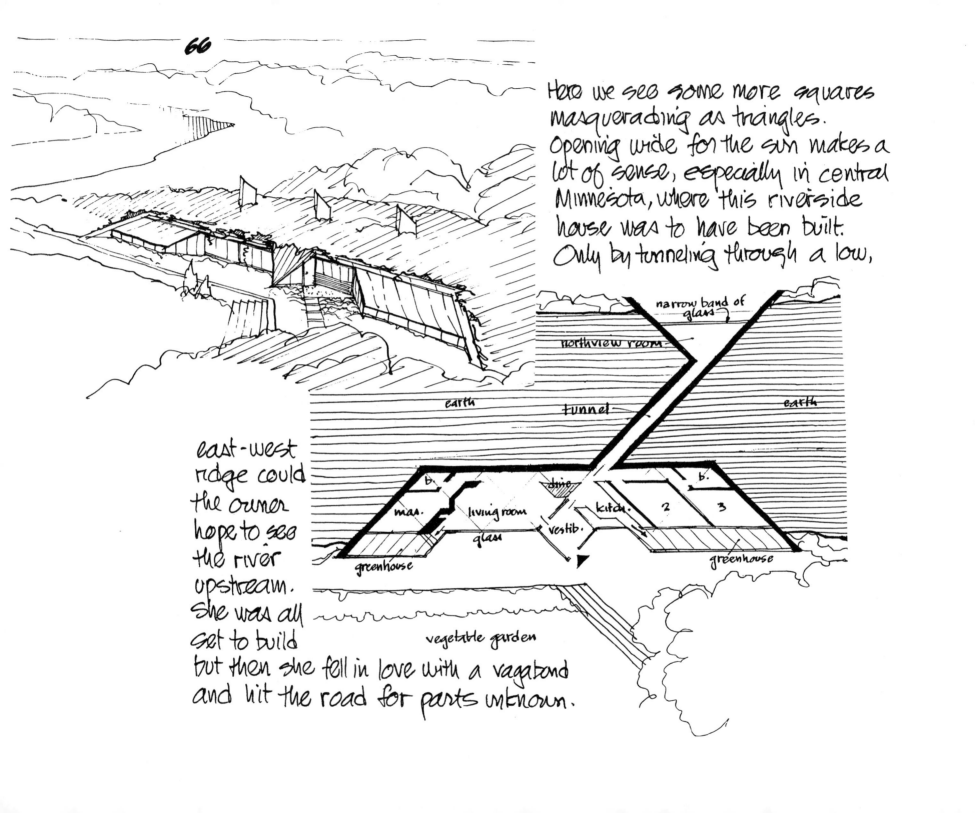

Here we see some more squares masquerading as triangles. Opening wide for the sun makes a lot of sense, especially in central Minnesota, where this riverside house was to have been built. Only by tunneling through a low,

east-west ridge could the owner hope to see the river upstream. She was all set to build but then she fell in love with a vagabond and hit the road for parts unknown.

narrow band of glass

northview room

earth

tunnel

earth

b.

mas.

living room

dine

glass

vestib.

kitch.

2

3

b.

greenhouse

greenhouse

vegetable garden

Architects love stairways – which are absolute barriers to the handicapped – and chimneys – which are notorious heat-wasters, especially
when hitched to fireplaces.
We love our fires, though,
and let them go only with
reluctance.

Could occasional open fires
crackling on the hearth
be forgiven by the goddess
of environment if we did
a lot of other things right?

There are times
when it seems that an
hour or so in front of a
cheery blaze is like money in
the bank … the spiritual bank,
that is. But if you say that
fires have to go, I'll bow to
your judgment.

How about a _half_ hour?

this is
the way
housing
developments
may look
if we adopt
environmental
building
codes

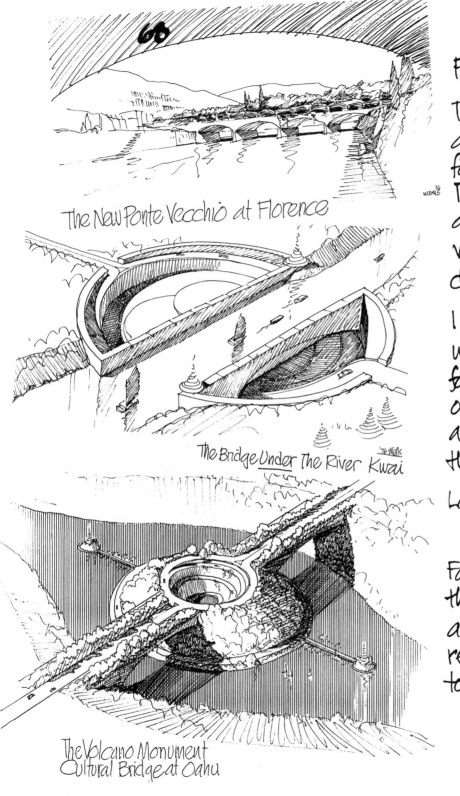

The New Ponte Vecchio at Florence

The Bridge _Under_ The River Kwai    '76 Wells

The Volcano Monument
Cultural Bridge at Oahu

Fantasy time.

The little cities of Fargo, North Dakota, and Moorhead, Minnesota, as you know, face each other across the Red River of the North. Back in the seventies, a joint announcement was made: they would invite submissions in a competition for the design of a new bridge linking the cities.

I offered them several suggestions, of which these were only a few, but they failed to see genius when it was right in front of them, awarding the prize instead to an architect named Michael Graves. Well, they had their chance — and blew it.

Last I heard, the bridge had not been built.


Fantasy time II: Do you think that all the genetic manipulation now going on among the mad scientists of the world's research labs will ever give us the ability to grow our buildings organically? It's not inconceivable that such things could happen. I'm leery of genetic manipulation in general. There are bound to be disasters along the way, when the wrong kinds of organisms get out of the labs, but if we could ever learn restraint...!

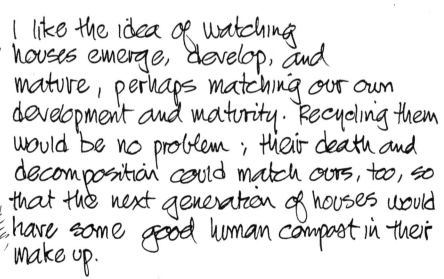

I like the idea of watching houses emerge, develop, and mature, perhaps matching our own development and maturity. Recycling them would be no problem; their death and decomposition could match ours, too, so that the next generation of houses would have some good human compost in their make up.

Talk about recycling! I didn't realize till I compared this design, just now, with the one on the next page how closely related they are. This was a proposal for a house at Wellfleet, here on Cape Cod. The road was at the top. A beautiful tidal marsh wasn't far from the bottom. A narrow step-down house was the result.

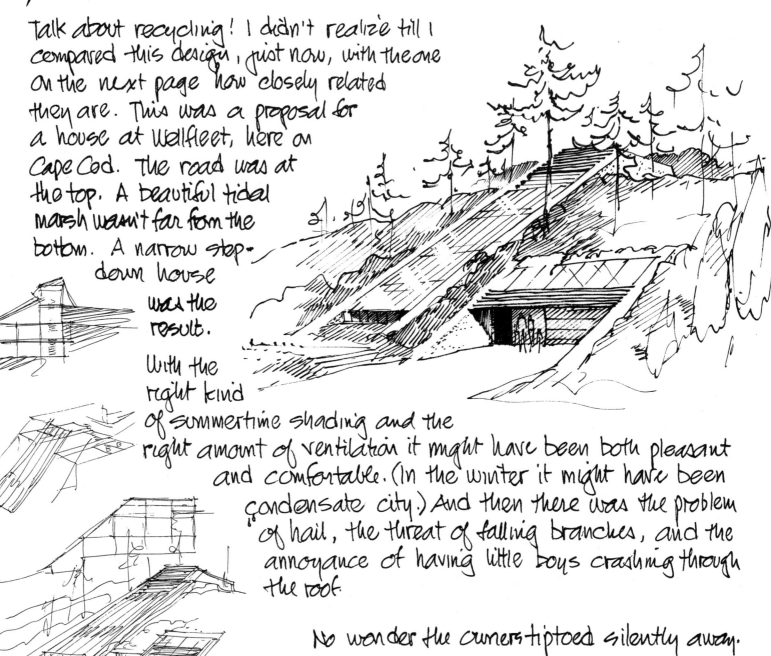

With the right kind of summertime shading and the right amount of ventilation it might have been both pleasant and comfortable. (In the winter it might have been condensate city.) And then there was the problem of hail, the threat of falling branches, and the annoyance of having little boys crashing through the roof.

No wonder the owners tiptoed silently away.

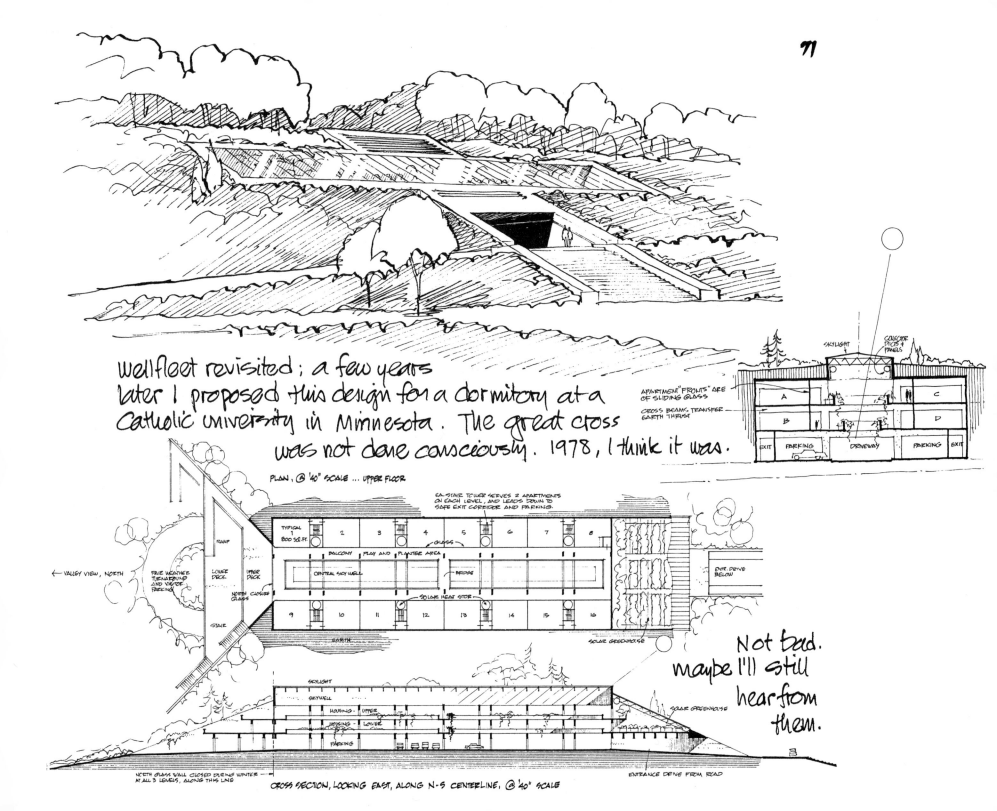

wellfleet revisited; a few years
later I proposed this design for a dormitory at a
Catholic university in Minnesota. The great cross
was not done consciously. 1978, I think it was.

SKYLIGHT — COLLECTOR RACKS & PANELS

APARTMENT "FRONTS" ARE OF SLIDING GLASS

CROSS BEAMS, TRANSFER EARTH THRUST

| A | | C |
| B | | D |
| EXIT | PARKING | DRIVEWAY | PARKING | EXIT |

PLAN, @ '40" SCALE ... UPPER FLOOR

EA STAIR TOWER SERVES 2 APARTMENTS ON EACH LEVEL, AND LEADS DOWN TO SAFE EXIT CORRIDOR AND PARKING.

← VALLEY VIEW, NORTH

FAIR WEATHER TURNAROUND AND VISITOR PARKING

RAMP

LOWER DECK — UPPER DECK

NORTH CLOSURE GLASS

STAIR

TYPICAL 1 800 SQ. FT.  2  3  4  5  6  7  8

GLASS

BALCONY PLAY AND PLANTER AREA

CENTRAL SKY WELL      BRIDGE

SOLAR HEAT STOR.

9  10  11  12  13  14  15  16

EARTH

SOLAR GREENHOUSE

ENTR. DRIVE BELOW

Not bad.
maybe I'll still
hear from
them.

SKYLIGHT
SKYWELL
HOUSING - UPPER
HOUSING - LOWER
PARKING

SOLAR GREENHOUSE

NORTH GLASS WALL CLOSED DURING WINTER AT ALL 3 LEVELS, ALONG THIS LINE

ENTRANCE DRIVE FROM ROAD

CROSS SECTION, LOOKING EAST, ALONG N-S CENTERLINE, @ '40" SCALE

Henry Ford's home in Dearborn, Michigan, was on an estate called Fairlane. The estate is now the Dearborn campus of the University of Michigan.

In 1979, when it was time to build a new environmental interpretation center, the university people reached all the way to Cape Cod for help.

After touring the campus and studying all the drawings they gave me, I proposed a building that sat astride a new pedestrian way leading from the heart of the campus to the woods along the river. To get to them, the main campus road had to be crossed, and the grades favored a pedestrian tunnel beneath that road.

This is a view from what I suppose you'd call the back of the proposed building through the tunnel and into the woods.

If I may refer you now to the site plan at right you'll see how it was arranged, and how another campus road was to have been diverted around the west side of the new

THE UNIVERSITY OF MICHIGAN - DEARBORN
**Environmental Interpretation Center**

THE FAIR LANE TUNNEL

building. The main entrance, shown here (and in an earlier design on the next page) was to have been entered from that west (campus) side.

Earth cover, natural plantings, solar heat, task lighting... even an organic vegetable garden... all were combined in the hope that the building would not only do good things but _say_ them.

THE UNIVERSITY OF MICHIGAN - DEARBORN
**Environmental Interpretation Center**

architecturally, as well. Ah, 'twas a lovely dream that slowly faded, as did so many of the rest, as funds dried up and the controllers of the moneybags turned to what they saw as more pressing needs.

NATIVE PLANTS ON BANKS SLOPED 1:2.5

ALCOVE FOR BIKES IN RETAINING WALL

(EXISTING CONTOURS)

MAIN ENTRANCE

NEW BUILDING
FLOOR ELEVATION : 5.0'
ROOFTOP SOIL : ± 25.0'

DIVERT ROAD

FAIR LANE

(TUNNEL)

COMPOST

FOOD

TO NAT. AREA

SLOT CUT THROUGH WOODS

EXISTING WALK TO PONY BARN PARKING LOT

THE UNIVERSITY OF MICHIGAN - DEARBORN
**Environmental Interpretation Center**

N

( ● = 7-11-79 REVISIONS )

0    50    100    150    200 FEET

PARTIAL SITE PLAN II

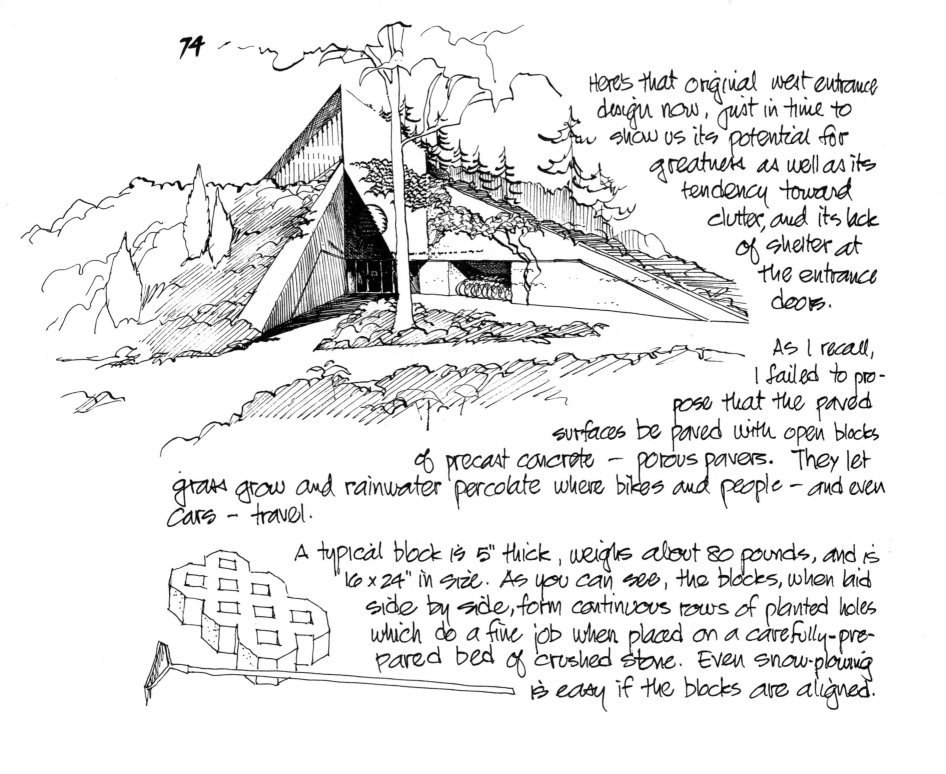

Here's that original west entrance design now, just in time to show us its potential for greatness as well as its tendency toward clutter, and its lack of shelter at the entrance doors.

As I recall, I failed to propose that the paved surfaces be paved with open blocks of precast concrete — porous pavers. They let grass grow and rainwater percolate where bikes and people — and even cars — travel.

A typical block is 5" thick, weighs about 80 pounds, and is 16 x 24" in size. As you can see, the blocks, when laid side by side, form continuous rows of planted holes which do a fine job when placed on a carefully-prepared bed of crushed stone. Even snow-plowing is easy if the blocks are aligned.

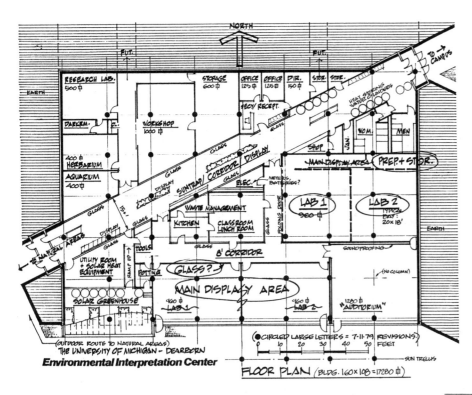

RESEARCH LAB.
500 ⊕

DARKRM.

400 ⊕
HERBARIUM

AQUARIUM
400 ⊕

STORAGE
600 ⊕

OFFICE 125 ⊕   OFFICE 125 ⊕   DIR. 150 ⊕   STOR.   STOR.

RECV. RECEPT.

HEAT STORING WATER CYLINDERS

WORKSHOP
1000 ⊕

SUNTRAP  CORRIDOR  DISPLAY

WASTE MANAGEMENT

KITCHEN

CLASSROOM LUNCH ROOM

SHOP  ELEC.

MAIN DISPLAY AREA   PREP.+ STOR.

LAB 1 960 ⊕

LAB 2 (TYPICAL BAY 20 × 18')

METERS/ BATTERIES?

UTILITY ROOM + SOLAR HEAT EQUIPMENT

TOOLS

POTTING

GLASS?

8' CORRIDOR

MAIN DISPLAY AREA

960 ⊕ LAB 1

960 ⊕ LAB 2

"1280 ⊕ AUDITORIUM"

(NO COLUMN)

SOUNDPROOFING

SOLAR GREENHOUSE

(OUTDOOR ROUTE TO NATURAL AREAS)

(●CIRCLED LARGE LETTERS = 7-11-79 REVISIONS.)
0  10  20  30  40  50  FEET

SUN TRELLIS

**THE UNIVERSITY OF MICHIGAN – DEARBORN**
**Environmental Interpretation Center**

FLOOR PLAN (BLDG. 160 × 108 = 17280 ⊕)

I'm afraid the only floor plan I can show you is this one with revisions marked on it. At least it will show you the campus-to-natural-areas axis as well as the use of insulation outside the concrete walls of the structure.

This lower plan is a day-lighting diagram which, I notice now, would have left the Interpretation Center's director in the dark. Let's revise that right now be-fore anyone else notices. All the other shaded areas needed, or could live with, artificial lighting.

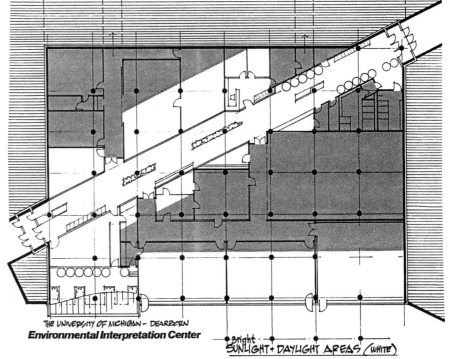

**THE UNIVERSITY OF MICHIGAN – DEARBORN**
**Environmental Interpretation Center**

· Bright ·
SUNLIGHT + DAYLIGHT AREAS (WHITE)

THE UNIVERSITY OF MICHIGAN - DEARBORN
**Environmental Interpretation Center**

CORRIDOR, LOOKING EAST

The idea was to use a frame of giant timbers. There were several reasons: Everyone loves to see wood. Wood suggests the idea of renewable resources. And the huge columns would perhaps remind those who saw, and touched, them of the living treasures we so casually condemn each time we specify the use of wood. A 2×4, or a sheet of plywood, down at the lumber yard, is so unlike the leafy creatures we love to see in the forest we often forget its source and forget the cost, in damage to our west-coast woodlands, that results from all our lumber purchases.

These columns were not to be west coast imports, however, but rather the trunks of local trees cleared away to make room for the ever-spreading scourge of surface construction.

If underground architecture ever gets to the stage at which it could be called

THE UNIVERSITY OF MICHIGAN - DEARBORN
**Environmental Interpretation Center**

THE SCALE OF THE SPACES

ever-spreading, it will be hard to call it a scourge as well. All construction causes land damage but underground architecture can heal the wounds, and in many cases can improve the health of the land, by getting the recuperation off to a good start and then standing back and letting the land work its wonders without further molestation, if you'll forgive the expression.

THE UNIVERSITY OF MICHIGAN - DEARBORN
**Environmental Interpretation Center**

CORRIDOR WINDOWS ABOVE ROOFTOP PLANTING.
AIR-TYPE SOLAR COLLECTORS ABOVE WINDOWS BELOW.
SOUTH/SOLAR FACADE

And so, as they say in the travelogues,
as the sun sinks slowly in the west,
we sail away from this lovely island
of dreams to the next few islands, which,
as it turned out, were made of dreams as well.

THE UNIVERSITY OF MICHIGAN - DEARBORN
**Environmental Interpretation Center**

DIAGONAL DISPLAY CORRIDOR
HAS 20'+ HEIGHT WITH CONTINUOUS 10' HIGH WINDOWS
(INSULATED AT NIGHT) FOR SOLAR GAIN, CENTER-OF-
BUILDING DAYLIGHTING, AND SUMMER VENTILATION.
SUN-WARMED AIR FROM COLLECTORS ON SOUTH FACADE, FROM
GREENHOUSE, AND FROM HIGH CORRIDOR SPACE
IS DRAWN DOWN AND BLOWN THROUGH ROCK BED
BELOW FLOOR, FOR HEAT STORAGE. WATER CYLINDERS
IN GREENHOUSE AND CORRIDOR STORE ADDITIONAL HEAT.
ELEVEN-FOOT-TALL WOOD COLUMNS, ABOUT 30" IN DIAMETER,
SUPPORT MASSIVE TIMBERS CARRYING ROOFTOP SOIL.
ENTIRE STRUCTURE IS WATERPROOFED AND
WRAPPED WITH EXTERIOR INSULATION BOARD.
TIMBER STRUCTURE EXTENDS BEYOND SOUTH FACADE
(RIGHT) TO FORM SUMMER SUN SHADE.
NATIVE PLANTS IN DEEP MULCH
COVER ROOF, SLOPES, AND
MUCH OF SITE. FENCES HIDDEN IN LANDSCAPING
PREVENT FALLS FROM ROOF EDGES.

CROSS SECTION LOOKING EAST

This plan, too, is just another square one, masquerading as an angled design.

I love excuses to walk out of doors, and these clients said they did, too. That's why the carport was to have been reached by way of a 50-

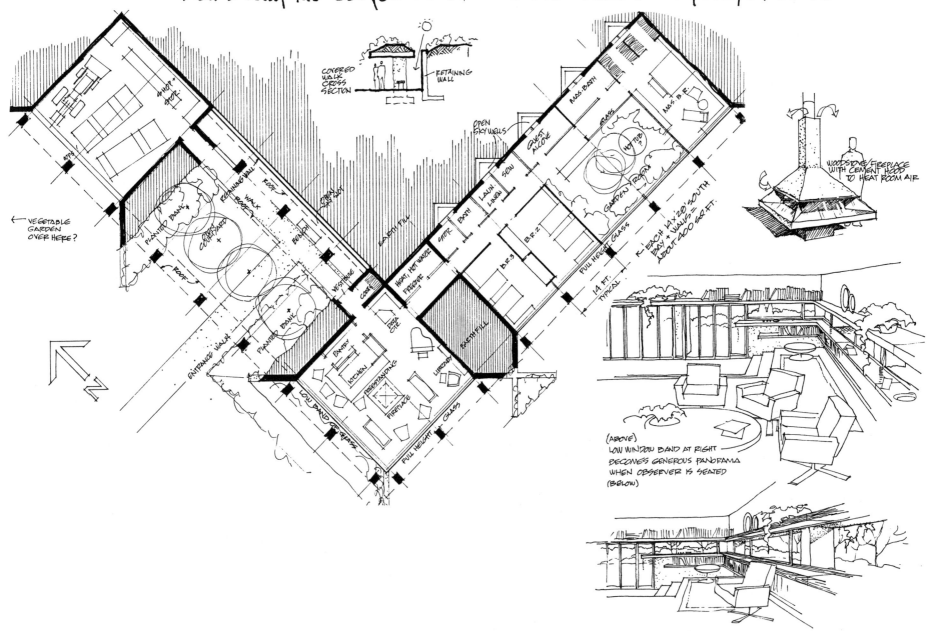

COVERED WALK CROSS SECTION

RETAINING WALL

← VEGETABLE GARDEN OVER HERE?

WOODSTOVE/FIREPLACE WITH CEMENT HOOD TO HEAT ROOM AIR

(ABOVE)
LOW WINDOW BAND AT RIGHT BECOMES GENEROUS PANORAMA WHEN OBSERVER IS SEATED
(BELOW)

odd-foot breezeway across the entry court. The site sloped down to the south, there was a lovely old avenue of deciduous trees through which the distant view was to be seen, and the plan was accepted with enthusiasm. The owners even liked the slit window at sit-down height along the west side of the living room.

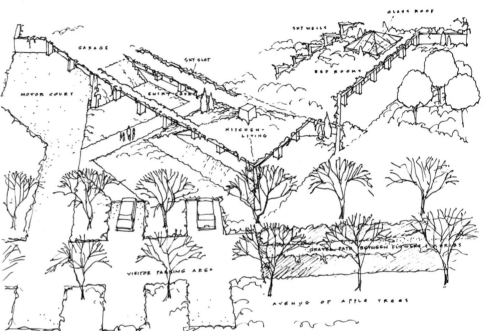

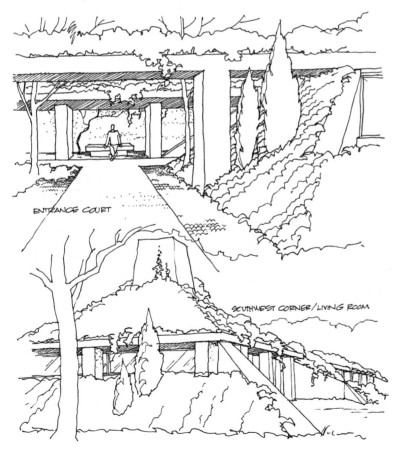

ENTRANCE COURT

SOUTHWEST CORNER/LIVING ROOM

Well, hang on, Mac, we'll be getting to some live ones in a page or two.

But first, we have this hillside solar earth shelter near Bradford, Pennsylvania, that never got any further. It was to have been part of a little bicycling community at which all the houses — ten of them, as I recall — would be strung along a horizontal path the main purpose of which was not to avoid having gentle slopes so much, as to express, architecturally, the things about land husbandry that similar horizontals in contour plowing express.

Philadelphia was, for a while, to have been the center of the 1976 Bicentennial festivities. I did this proposal for the other side of the river, for poor old Camden, New Jersey.

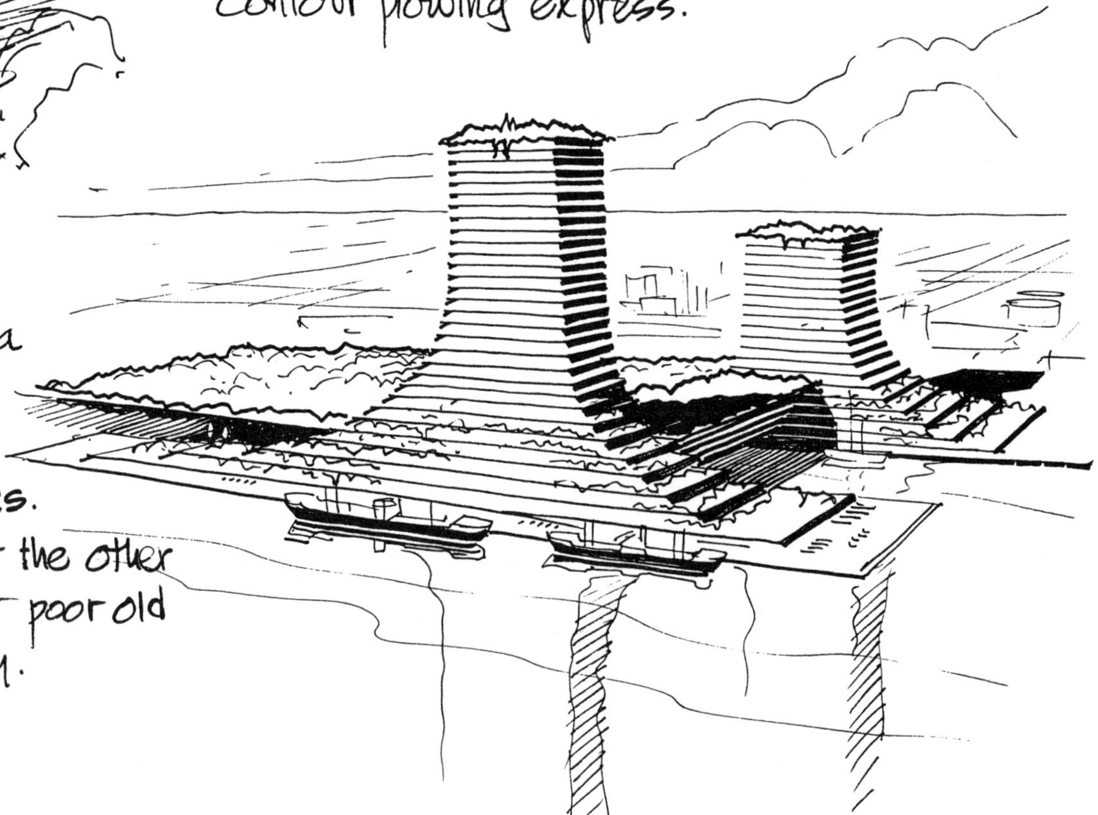

What was that thing, anyway?... a pair of office towers, or hotels, or what?
You name it; that's what it was to have been.

Getting back down to earth again, we have, first, the sniffer duct, an idea that's
worked successfully for me in several buildings. It simply
pulls solar (or otherwise) heated air down from ceiling
level, before it's wasted, and pushes it through under-
slab air tubes, storing the warmth in the floor-mass
before the air emerges, ready to go around again.
I didn't use insulation below the slab in my latest
building. My hope and belief is that the great
mass of earth below will gradually warm up a bit and
carry the building through the coldest of cloudy cold spells.

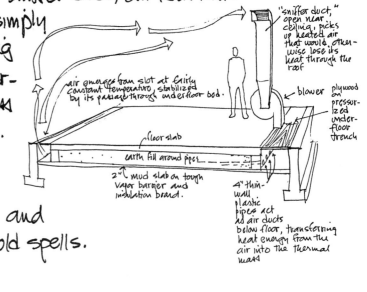

"sniffer duct," open near ceiling, picks up heated air that would otherwise lose its heat through the roof

air emerges from slot at fairly constant temperature, stabilized by its passage through underfloor bed.

blower

plywood

pressurized underfloor trench

floor slab

earth fill around pipes

2" mud slab on tough vapor barrier and insulation board.

4" thin-wall plastic pipes act as air ducts below floor, transferring heat energy from the air into the thermal mass

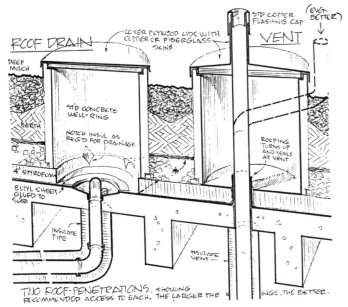

ROOF DRAIN

COVER PLYWOOD LIDS WITH COPPER OR FIBERGLASS SKINS

STD COPPER FLASHING CAP

(EVEN BETTER)

VENT

DEEP MULCH

STD CONCRETE WELL-RING

NOTCH INSUL AS REQ'D FOR DRAINAGE

EARTH

ROOFING TURNS UP AND SEALS AT VENT

4" STYROFOAM

BUTYL SHEET GLUED TO SLAB

INSULATE PIPE

INSULATE VENT

TWO ROOF-PENETRATIONS, SHOWING RECOMMENDED ACCESS TO EACH. THE LARGER THE ___ INGS, THE BETTER.

It's nice to be able to get to roof penetrations
without having to dig for them, don't you think?

This is my showpiece, or, I should say, this will be my showpiece.

Launched in 1971, "Locust Hill" at Raven Rocks, near Beallsville in eastern Ohio, is still under construction. Now in its 20th year, the great hillside house/office/workplace will be ready, this season, to receive its second floor. As you can imagine, there were twists and turns along the way.

In the early Seventies, the architect, still not persuaded that

LOCUST HILL
CA. 1980

solar heating would really work,
sited the house on an east-facing hillside, and several foundations were poured before energy expert Bruce Anderson and his company.

ENTRANCE

VISITOR DROP-OFF

Total Environmental Action, got the owners to abandon the job. That they did so with good humor says a lot about the delightful people who've come to be among my closest friends.

Four people have been most directly involved in the Raven Rocks project but they've had a lot of help from the others in the 18 or 20 member group. The four: Chris Joyner, Don Hartley, Tim Starbuck, and Warren Stetzel. Over the years, Warren and I have traded hundreds of letters on every subject from the U.S.

backed atrocities in Central America to the world environmental crisis, not to mention all the house details that have been proposed, discarded or refined, and worked into the project.

I will no doubt be given credit for designing Locust Hill but all the most important aspects of it have come from Raven Rocks. Hoping to make use of the very best thinking on what I call Gentle Architecture, they will not hesitate to travel halfway across the country in their VW bus to see a promising

experiment. Talk about open minds! They think nothing of changing plans in midstream (or however you say it) or tearing out a beautifully-completed piece of work if they think that in the long run (500 years or so) the building will serve as a better example if it incorporates more efficient features.

The Raven Rocks people have achieved a kind of self-sufficiency already, raising mouth-wateringly beautiful food in their lush gardens, repairing and

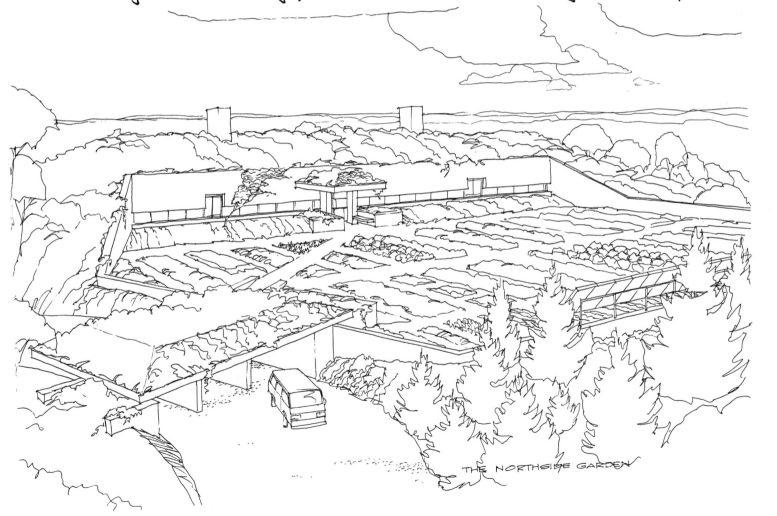

THE NORTHSIDE GARDEN

sometimes even fabricating parts for their equipment. They hope, some-day, by the use of photovoltaics, to cut free of the electric lines that now power their temporary quarters on the site.

"Are they millionaires?" people have asked me. Far from it. They run a smallish concrete company, and they raise and sell Christmas trees (prize specimens, naturally, free of pesticides and even fertilizers). Money is not the main factor when determination is involved. Of course their determination is augmented by high intelligence, a world perspective, unfailing good humor, enjoyment of life, and sheer hard work. They think nothing, for instance, of staying up most of the night

finishing concrete slabs if weather conditions, available time, and other factors indicate that that's the best thing to do.

UPPER FLOOR, NEAR THE SOUTH WALL

My daughter, Kappy, says I draw old-fashioned chairs. They don't look old-fashioned to me. Maybe 1950-ish, but is that old? I've been drawing Paul McCobb-ish chairs for 40 years now, not seeing, until she reminded me, that I've been standing still and the world's been moving by. So please don't be put off by my furnishings. Think instead about the often-diffused sunlight of eastern Ohio coming in through these specially-glazed, doubly-insulated windows and being trapped by them to warm the great masses of concrete nestled into the hillside. Think about the hundreds of acres of poetically beautiful ravines and forests out there, all land that the Raven Rocks people saved from the strip-miners with just minutes to spare.

May every architect have clients like the Raven Rocks group at least once in his or her career!

LOOKING SOUTH FROM THE KITCHEN AT LOCUST HILL

(Raven Rocks, cont'd)

Just down the lane from Locust Hill, Raven Rocks couple Mary and Rich Sidwell are building, too, at a considerably faster pace than that of their neighbors. Two years or so and they're putting the roof on already! Not having to duplicate a lot of the Locust Hill research helped, as did the construction experience gained over there.

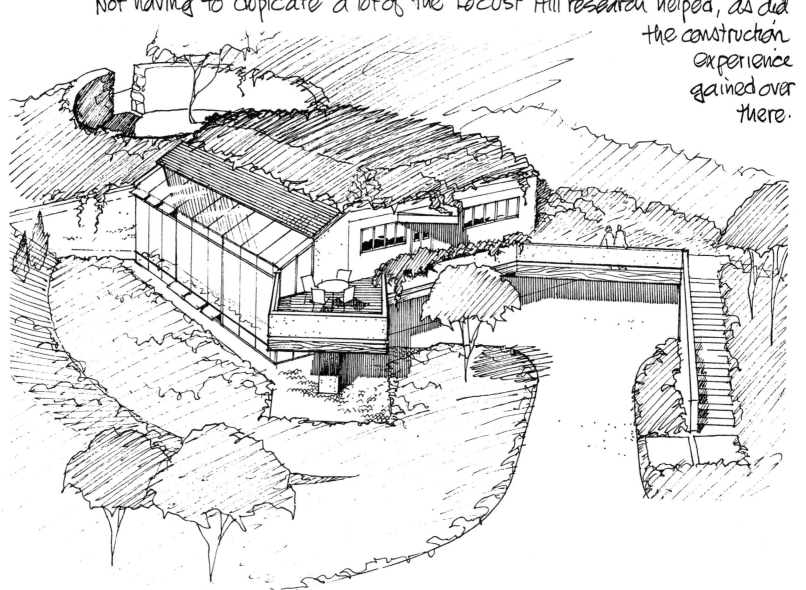

Did you notice the carport tucked in underground below the Sidwells as they take a break for a moment and stand at the rail?

Clivus's composting toilets have been used at all the Raven Rocks households for years, producing rich compost while the rest of us have been flushing our wastes into rivers and bays, or into fragile soils, as we do here on Cape Cod. We continue this insane practice even though the clean-up of nearby Boston Harbor is predicted to cost billions. I finally got a Clivus system approved and installed here in Brewster, but what a fight it took! The toughest adversary: the state Department of <u>Environmental Quality Engineering</u>!

But we all know that the wheels of progress turn slowly. My wheels of greenhouse-design progress for the Sidwells turned slowly enough. These drawings represent some ———→ of the possibilities I proposed before being helped by the Sidwells in the direction of the design you see at left.

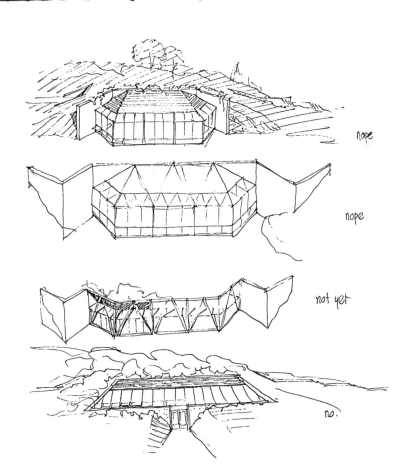

nope

nope

not yet

no.

Once these Raven Rocks buildings get finished, and their landscaping has settled in for a couple of years, I'm going to spend a lot of money on color film.

I suspect, and hope, I won't be alone.

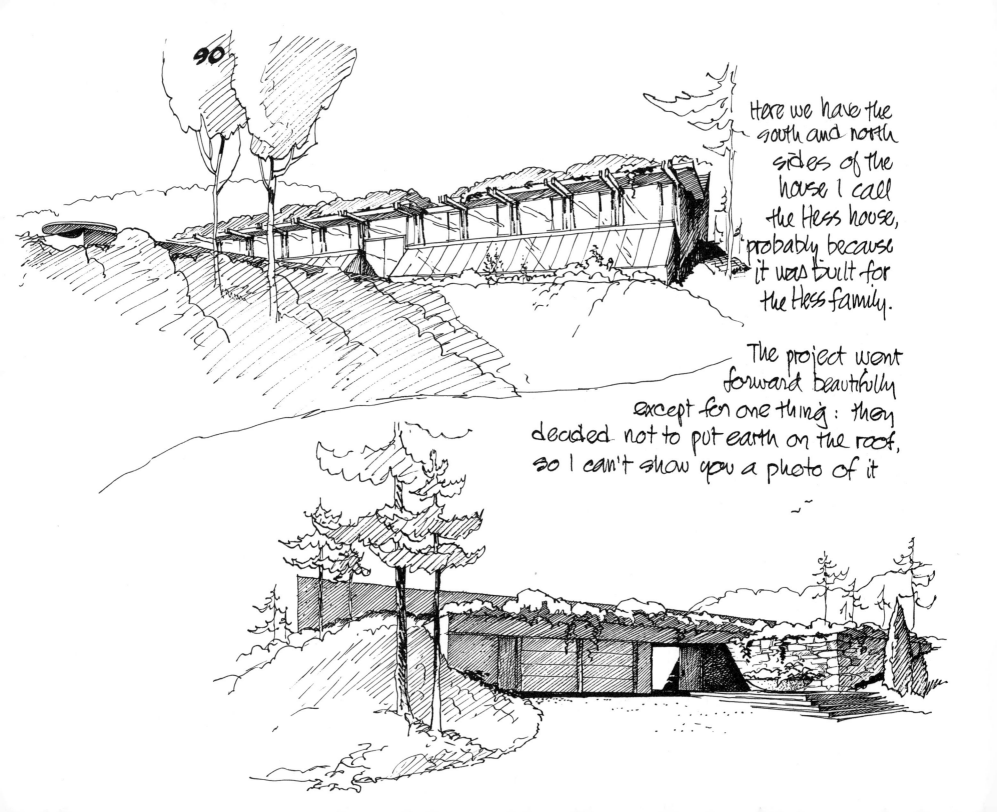

Here we have the south and north sides of the house I call the Hess house, probably because it was built for the Hess family.

The project went forward beautifully except for one thing: they decided not to put earth on the roof, so I can't show you a photo of it with glorious rooftop plantings overspilling the sides.

But as a solar house it performed extremely well, and I picked up a bit more drawing experience.

Trained as an engineer at Georgia Tech, I never spent a day in its architectural school,* and my architectural apprenticeship was spent in the office of a man who did nothing but Colonial houses. It was good drafting experience but since the floor plans all looked like this, my own early designs never seemed to have any strength. Slowly, I learned to hang buildings on simple repetitive structural skeletons.

*except when I was dating the architectural librarian.

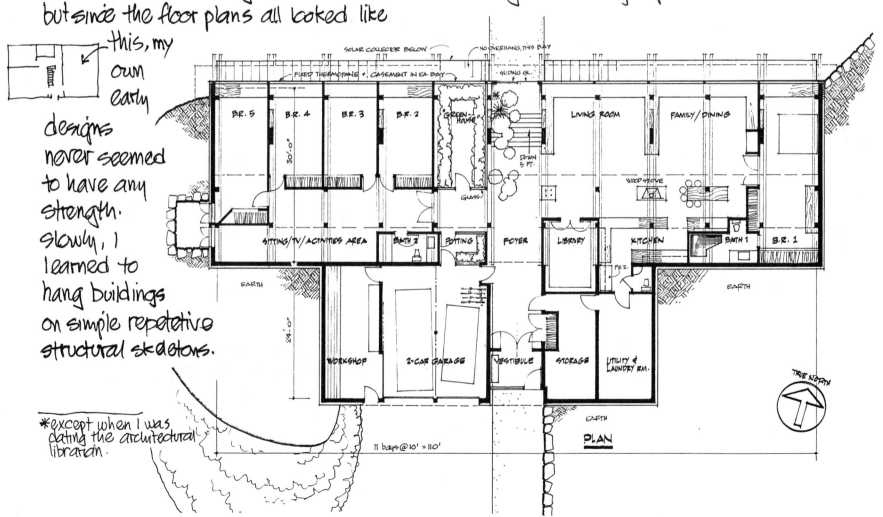

PLAN

This skeleton was a bold one, designed to carry the earth load that never came along. In the perspective at right you can see that the fireplace has been moved back against the wall (on p. 91 it was free-standing). Other than that, the drawings appear pretty much to agree with one another.

Just don't try to blow under-slab air through a rock bed. Fortunately for me — and them - the Hesses never used that kind of heat storage system. Neither did any of my other clients in those (ca. 1979) days. Dust, cobwebs, and dead mice are just a few of the rock bed problems about which I've been told.

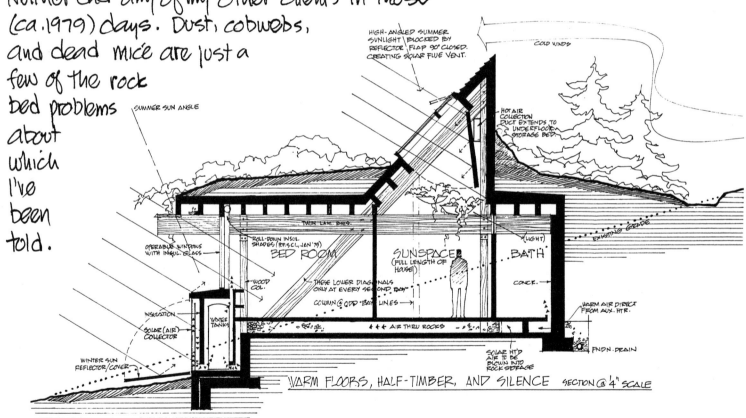

HIGH-ANGLED SUMMER SUNLIGHT BLOCKED BY REFLECTOR FLAP 90° CLOSED. CREATING SOLAR FLUE VENT.

COLD WINDS

SUMMER SUN ANGLE

HOT AIR COLLECTION DUCT EXTENDS TO UNDERFLOOR STORAGE BED.

EXISTING GRADE

TWIN LAM. BMS.

ROLL-DOWN INSUL. SHADES (POP.SCI., JAN '79)

OPERABLE WINDOWS WITH INSUL. GLASS

(LIGHT)

BED ROOM

SUNSPACE (FULL LENGTH OF HOUSE)

BATH

WOOD COL.

THESE LOWER DIAGONALS ONLY AT EVERY SECOND BAY

COLUMN @ ODD BAY LINES →

CONC.

INSULATION

SOLAR (AIR) COLLECTOR

WATER TANKS

WARM AIR DIRECT FROM AUX. HTR.

← ← ← AIR THRU ROCKS

FNDN. DRAIN

WINTER SUN REFLECTOR/COVER

SOLAR HT'D AIR TO BE BLOWN INTO ROCK STORAGE

WARM FLOORS, HALF-TIMBER, AND SILENCE    SECTION @ ¼" SCALE

(Slightly more modern chairs, but only slightly.)

cantilevered shelves have long been favored architectural devices with
me but here they have a practical side as well), preventing unwitting head-
bumpings on the sloping beams. When I do upper-room designs in the attics
of more conventional houses, I like to let the roof and floor planes
meet cleanly at a point. Cabinets or seats are always extended to
head-clearance height in such cases, to avoid the bumping problem.

Location: somewhere in eastern
Pennsylvania.

After 50 – 51 – years of living in New Jersey, and after almost 25 years of doing my share to contribute to its environment's downfall, I was able to move back into the best part of my past by moving to Cape Cod. My little self-published book, <u>Underground Designs</u>, was selling so well I was able to buy 23 acres of beautiful pine and oak woods, fronting on 3 ponds, for $78,000, cash! It didn't take long to find the best part of the tract: a high ridge overlooking the largest of the ponds. There wasn't another house visible in any direction. At night: not even a light.

The only trouble with that best part of the tract was that the ridge ran north-south (above), with the pond view to the east. The design solution: face south and tunnel through the ridge to a pond-view living room.

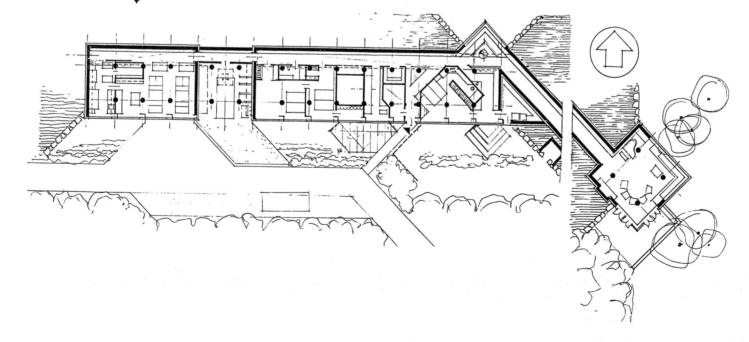

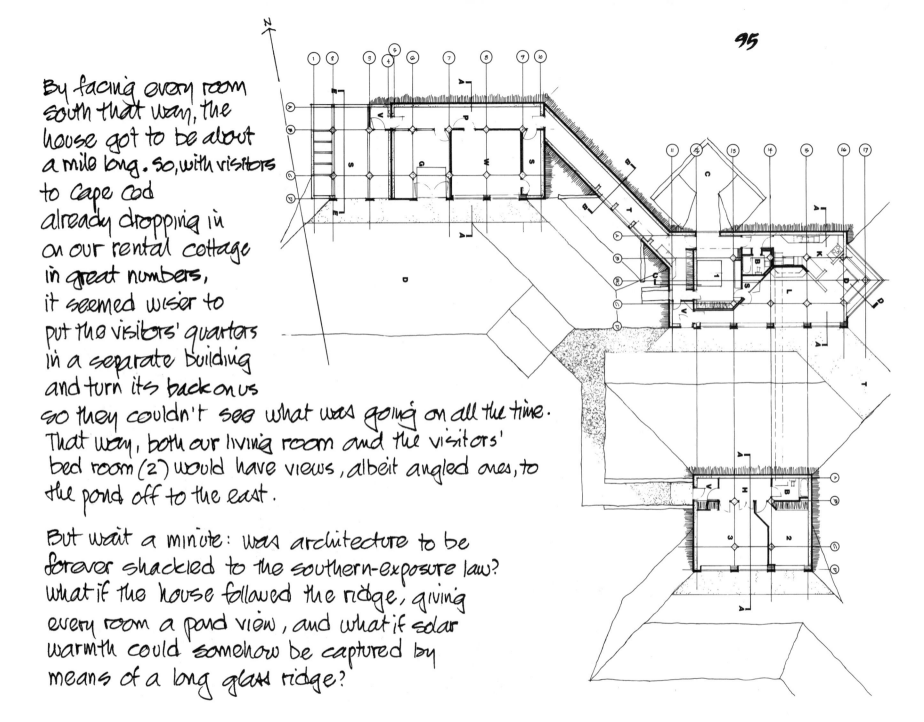

By facing every room south that way, the house got to be about a mile long. So, with visitors to Cape Cod already dropping in on our rental cottage in great numbers, it seemed wiser to put the visitors' quarters in a separate building and turn its back on us so they couldn't see what was going on all the time. That way, both our living room and the visitors' bed room (2) would have views, albeit angled ones, to the pond off to the east.

But wait a minute: was architecture to be forever shackled to the southern-exposure law? What if the house followed the ridge, giving every room a pond view, and what if solar warmth could somehow be captured by means of a long glass ridge?

West side perspective

So here it was, the ridge-line house ... living quarters to the left, guests and my office to the right. In the center, a glass-roofed — and unheated — foyer filled with plants hardy enough to survive winter nights on which temperatures could drop close to freezing.

Did it work? Truthfully, now. Yes, pretty well. The big double-glazed and window-quilted windows on the opposite side picked up a fair amount of early warmth; then the skylight did the job all through the middle of the day, and the high-up sniffer duct, right below the skylight, pulled the room-top warmth down and into the floor slab.

Cape Cod in the winter can have prolonged periods of raging winds off the ocean (9 miles from this site) with no sun visible for weeks. During such periods the little oil burner, combined with the effects of the great mass of insulated concrete and the earth shelter, was able to keep the house comfortable for a very low cost.

The main weakness of the house was its skylight design. After a few years the caulking in the wood members had begun to crack and admit water. And after those same few years I'd gotten sick of lifting the big winter-glazing panels (dotted line below) high up into the horizontal position and trying to bolt them into place while the weight of each panel was pressing on my head. A far better system would have employed permanent, reflective-surfaced insulation-board panels — one in each bay — that could be rotated into and out of position either at the tug of a cord or by the action of a little motor.

But the principle, facing east but managing to capture plenty of solar heat, was sound, in spite of the bugs in the design.

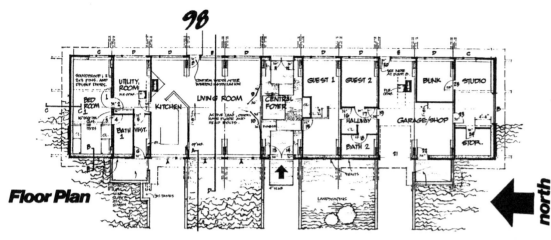

**Floor Plan**

The floor plan.

Each bay is 11' x 24', and there are 11 of them, bringing the total floor area to 7,692.4 square feet.

No, that's not right; let me try that again: 11 x 11 x 24 = 2904 square feet. It cost less than $50/sq. foot. Today, 1990, about ten years later, the cost would be more than double.

It was a nice house in a beautiful location, but troubles, other than architectural ones — or even financial ones — put the house in the hands of others, and it has been changed considerably as a result, its skylight removed and shingled over, its sniffer ducts gone, its rooms rearranged, and its garden circle bulldozed away.

I wouldn't be surprised to hear from the new owners at any time. "What are all these trenches in the floor?" they may ask, or, "why are there terra cotta flues coming up out of the plants in the foyer?"

I'll try to behave myself, if that occurs, and not make up any fantastic lies about nuclear reactor vents or mink-breeding tunnels.

After all, the house is only a mile away and I want to be a good neigh-

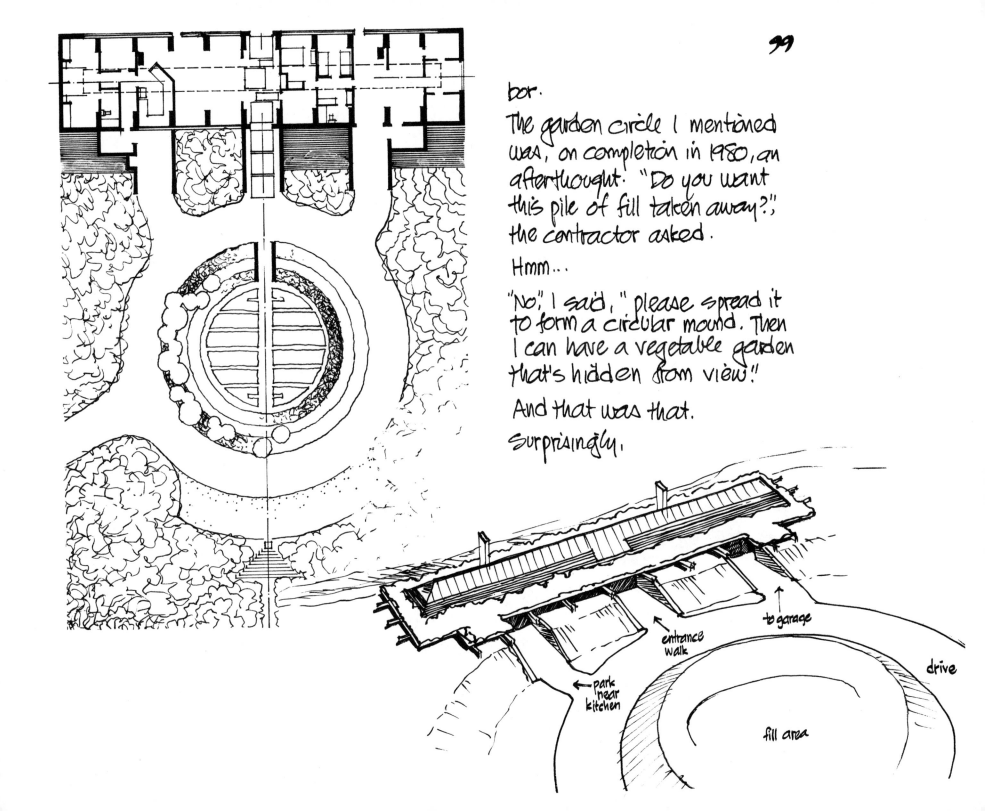

bor.

The garden circle I mentioned was, on completion in 1980, an afterthought. "Do you want this pile of fill taken away?," the contractor asked.

Hmm...

"No," I said, "please spread it to form a circular mound. Then I can have a vegetable garden that's hidden from view!"

And that was that.

Surprisingly.

to garage

drive

entrance walk

park near kitchen

fill area

it not only proved to be a handy spot for growing vegetables, it proved to have a much more stable temperature, probably because of the encircling earth mass, than any garden I'd worked before. In the fall, when local gardeners were having frost troubles, I wasn't. It was often weeks later when frost would have the nerve to enter the circle.

Our little furry friends in the forest never did have the nerve. While others complained of the damage done their gardens by rabbits, squirrels, muskrats, and deer, we couldn't complain of any. All I have to explain it is an amateur's theory: animals, which surely checked out the living salad in the big ring, felt they'd be unable to escape in a hurry and, as a result, were never quite tempted to sample the fare.

With amazing foresight, I devised little inverted pans to protect the vulnerable top surfaces of the projecting twin 3x12 pine collar ties. Each pan had an upturned flashing that went behind the fascia (at "x"). The wood was like new after 5 years.

But I never anticipated the air leakage all around the 3x12s where they passed out through the cement-stucco'd building wall (Y). During the first howling nor' easter in the winter of '80-'81, the drapes almost blew down from the force of the wind coming in all the cracks around the 3x12s. Caulking helped, later on, but as the members continued to shrink, and twist, new openings appeared.

There is no 100% solution, particularly if the wood checks, that is, splits harmlessly along its length. But if pieces of sheet metal are inserted into 1/4" deep kerfs (saw cuts), most of the air leakage due to shrinkage and twisting can be eliminated. The sheet metal occurs just at the outer face of the wall sheathing.

And now for a final look as we lift off and fly away, this view being from the south.

Don't miss
the photo pages!

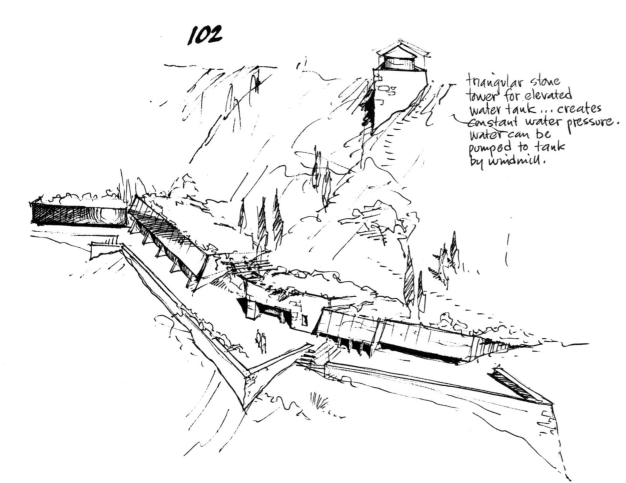

triangular stone tower for elevated water tank ... creates constant water pressure. water can be pumped to tank by windmill.

I feel just a little ashamed of this drawing, now that I see it again. It was my first response to a commission to build a solar, earth-covered addition to a house in Greece.

Imagine: greece! what a lot of impressions that were generated!

I'm embarrassed because, having been given the design of the existing building I failed to bow to its precedent and let a blocky rectangular theme run through all the rest.

Yes, there's a nice solar/hillside statement here, but if I missed the boat on the basics what good is all the rest? How could I do that to the Parthenon people?

Fortunately, the question was moot. Nothing ever came of the first exchange of letters.

then why are you wasting our time with all this nonsense?

Just in case the lesson is of use to you.

The Nature Museum; Charlotte, North Carolina. 1976

Now _there_ was an opportunity. Underground parking. Underground building. Solar energy. Natural plantings. Rainwater percolation. A nature-oriented client. Exhibits. Education. A downtown location. A willingness to experiment...

Whatever happened to that job, anyway?

Beats me. I suppose it was awarded to someone else, designed, built, and admired by all who saw it. I hope so. The people I met at the little building that formerly housed The Nature Museum deserved a good one. Their values were, to my mind, right on the money.

Maybe the existing church, there on the other corner of the block, would have been lent some ethical reinforcement by the museum. And, of course, maybe the museum would have been lent some by the church.

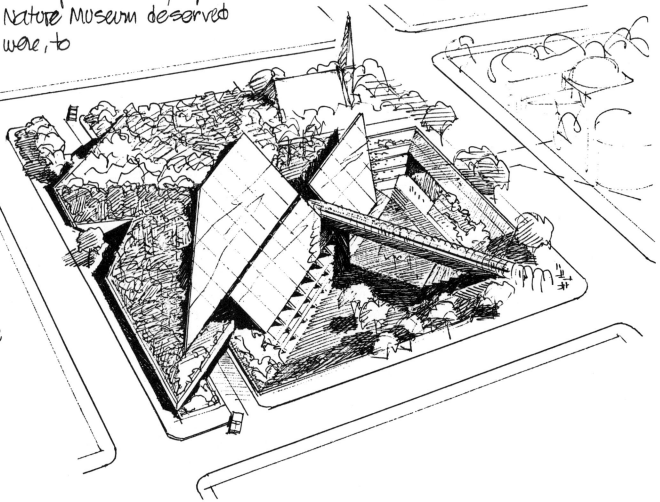

How's this for a simple floor plan? It's a cousin of the one I'd been playing with for years, finally to appear as the <u>Popular Science</u> house (pp.184.5) of April, 1989. A later version of this plan, before this project, like so many others, was abandoned, had additional rooms in what is shown here as an open-to-the-weather carport space. The extra space would undoubtedly have been useful but the nice outdoor separation — putting the kids, or the guests, off by themselves, not to mention the appeal of having a deep, inviting recess in the center of the facade — would, in my view, have been the better choice.

This went up to a vegetable garden on the gentle slope north of the house.

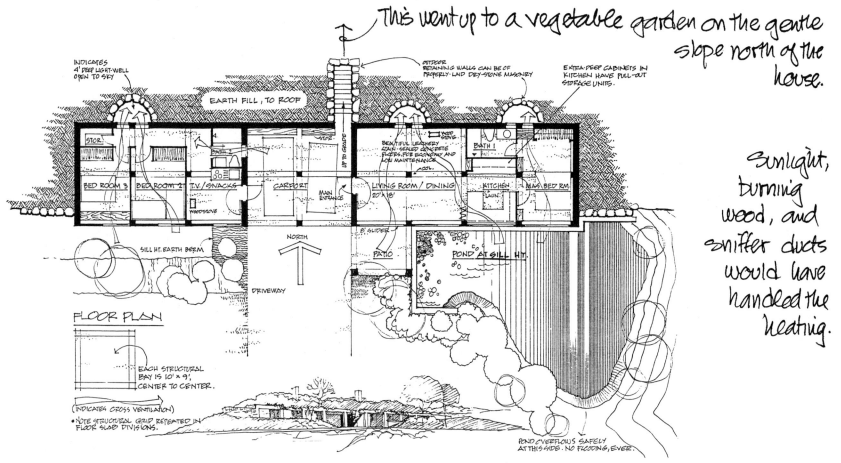

Sunlight, burning wood, and sniffer ducts would have handled the heating.

INDICATES 4' DEEP LIGHT-WELL OPEN TO SKY

OUTDOOR RETAINING WALLS CAN BE OF PROPERLY-LAID DRY-STONE MASONRY

EXTRA-DEEP CABINETS IN KITCHEN HAVE PULL-OUT STORAGE UNITS.

EARTH FILL, TO ROOF

STOR.

STOR.

WOOD STOVE

BEAUTIFUL LEATHERY STAIN-SEALED CONCRETE FLOORS FOR ECONOMY AND LOW MAINTENANCE.

BATH 1

BED ROOM 3

BED ROOM 2

BATH 2

T.V./SNACKS

CARPORT

UP TO GRADE

MAIN ENTRANCE

LIVING ROOM / DINING 20' x 18'

KITCHEN

LAUN.

MAS. BED RM.

WOODSTOVE

SILL HT. EARTH BERM

NORTH

8' SLIDER

PATIO

POND AT SILL HT.

DRIVEWAY

FLOOR PLAN

EACH STRUCTURAL BAY IS 10' x 9', CENTER TO CENTER.

(INDICATES CROSS VENTILATION)

• NOTE STRUCTURAL GRID REPEATED IN FLOOR SLAB DIVISIONS.

POND OVERFLOWS SAFELY AT THIS SIDE. NO FLOODING, EVER.

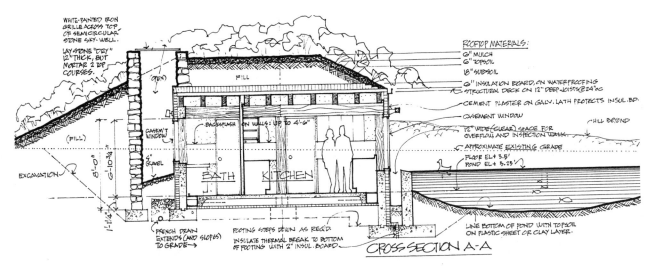

WHITE-PAINTED IRON GRILLE ACROSS TOP OF SEMICIRCULAR STONE SKY-WELL.

LAY STONE "DRY" 12" THICK, BUT MORTAR 2 TOP COURSES.

ROOFTOP MATERIALS:
6" MULCH
6" TOPSOIL
18" SUBSOIL
6" INSULATION BOARD, ON WATERPROOFING
STRUCTURAL DECK ON 12" DEEP JOISTS @ 24" OC
CEMENT PLASTER ON GALV. LATH PROTECTS INSUL. BD.
CASEMENT WINDOW
HILL BEYOND

(OPEN)
FILL
(FILL)

12" WIDE (CLEAR) SPACE FOR OVERFLOW AND INSPECTION WALK.
APPROXIMATE EXISTING GRADE
FLOOR EL + 3.5'
POND EL + 5.25'

CASEM'T WINDOW
EXCAVATION
BACKSPLASH ON WALLS: UP TO 4'-6"
GRAVEL
BATH   KITCHEN

8'-0"
6'-10¾"
1'-1¼"

FRENCH DRAIN EXTENDS (AND SLOPES) TO GRADE→
FOOTING STEPS DOWN AS REQ'D.
INSULATE THERMAL BREAK TO BOTTOM OF FOOTING WITH 2" INSUL. BOARD.
LINE BOTTOM OF POND WITH TOPSOIL ON PLASTIC SHEET OR CLAY LAYER.

CROSS SECTION A-A

You wouldn't want to get stuck in that narrow overflow slot between the pond and the house! Better to make it, say, 24" wide. The timber trellis, shown below, was to have covered only the little patio but if the posts had tiptoed right across the pond, shading all the east-end rooms, it might have been more effective — and dramatic.

A problem to consider: if the last (northernmost) purlin (sub-beam), shown resting on the concrete wall, shrank ½" in height, and the other purlins (and the main beam supporting them) shrank a total of 1", would water forever be trapped in/on an underground roof puddle? Would it matter?

Better slope the roof a little.

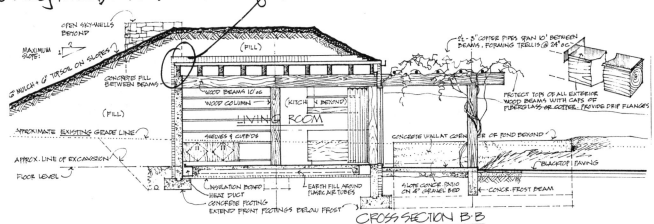

OPEN SKY-WELLS BEYOND

MAXIMUM SLOPE: 1 / 2

6" MULCH + 6" TOPSOIL ON SLOPES
CONCRETE FILL BETWEEN BEAMS
(FILL)
(FILL)

2½-3" COPPER PIPES SPAN 10' BETWEEN BEAMS, FORMING TRELLIS @ 24" OC

WOOD BEAMS 10' OC
WOOD COLUMN   (KITCHEN BEYOND)
LIVING ROOM
SHELVES & CUB'DS

APPROXIMATE EXISTING GRADE LINE
APPROX. LINE OF EXCAVATION
FLOOR LEVEL

PROTECT TOPS OF ALL EXTERIOR WOOD BEAMS WITH CAPS OF FIBERGLASS OR COPPER. PROVIDE DRIP FLANGES

CONCRETE WALL AT CORNER OF POND BEYOND
BLACKTOP PAVING

INSULATION BOARD
HEAT DUCT
CONCRETE FOOTING
EXTEND FRONT FOOTINGS BELOW FROST
EARTH FILL AROUND PLASTIC AIR TUBES
SLOPE CONCR. PATIO ON 4" GRAVEL BED
CONCR. FROST BEAM

CROSS SECTION B-B

If you can't bury them, berm them, isn't that the rule? When I was asked to design a restaurant and a bank building at an office "park" surrounding a quarter-mile long lake, I knew, from

A RESTAURANT THAT LOOKS RIGHT DOWN THE LAKE, EXPRESSING, IN ITS FORM, THE IDEAS OF "VIEW," "SOLAR ENERGY," AND "LAND HUSBANDRY."

I SENT THOSE NEWLYWEDS UP ONTO THE SLOPE TO SHOW YOU HOW BIG THE DINING ROOM WINDOW-BAND IS.

having tried to sell the idea there before, that earth-covered roofs would not be accepted. All I could do was point in the direction of earthiness, with some plantings on one roof and landscaped slopes up to the other.

Writing about roofs reminds me that I've said very little about the water-proofing of earth-covered roofs, so, if I don't mention it in the next few pages, please remind me.

NOT JUST ANOTHER BOX-BUILDING ON A BUSY STREET CORNER BUT AN EARTH-OBJECT; PART OF THE LAKESIDE WOODS, INVITING ITS CUSTOMERS TO A BIT OF SOLIDITY AND PEACE.

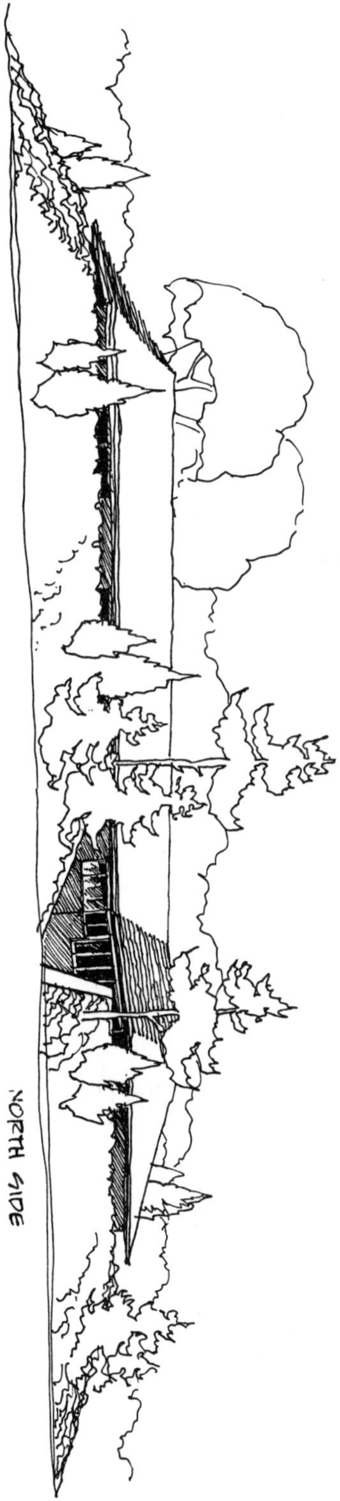

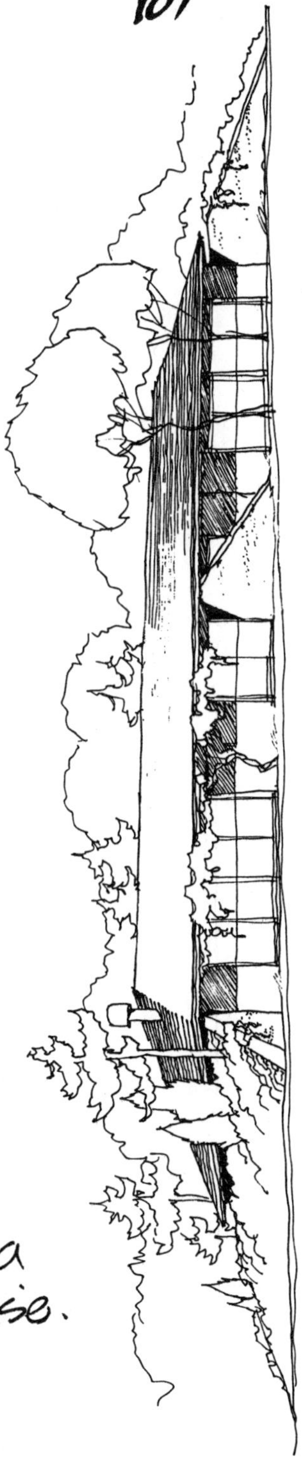

NORTH SIDE

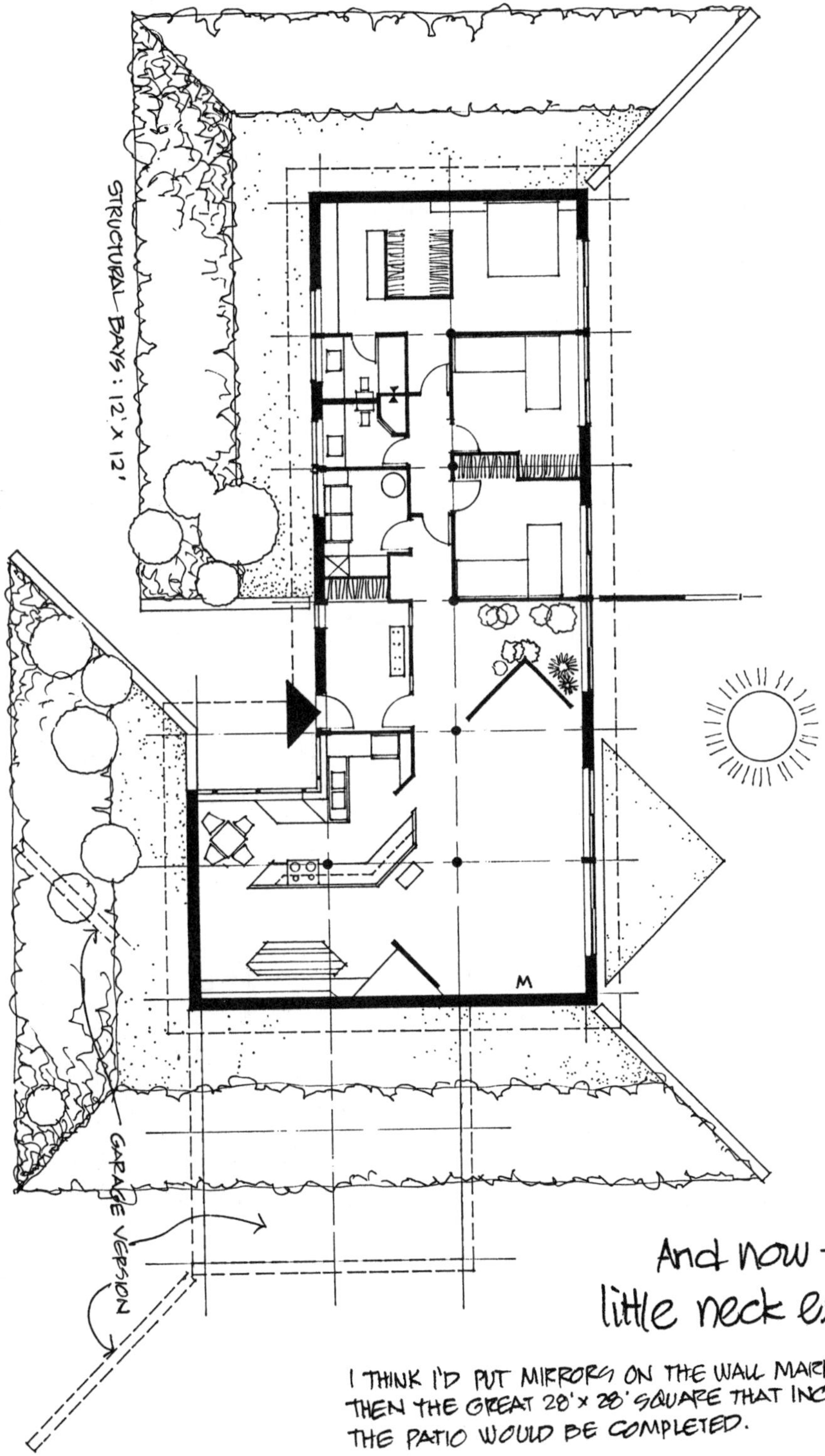

SOUTH SIDE

STRUCTURAL BAYS : 12' x 12'

GARAGE VERSION

M

And now for a
little neck exercise.

I THINK I'D PUT MIRRORS ON THE WALL MARKED "M."
THEN THE GREAT 28' x 28' SQUARE THAT INCLUDES
THE PATIO WOULD BE COMPLETED.

Cape Cod is a lovely peninsula of sea and sun, and forests of pine that are being stripped away at a frightening rate to make room for thousands of phony Cape Cod cottages, and acres of shopping centers that look like phony houses.

I've had two chances to build a home and office for my wife and myself, and I'm more determined this time, perhaps, than I was the first time, to resist the new Cape Cod tradition.

My wife, Karen, and I are just now completing what we call the gallery wing of that second Cape Cod house, and these drawings illustrate its evolution.

The new gallery is barely recognizable in this 1985 version but its basic 60'x 20' underground shape has never changed.

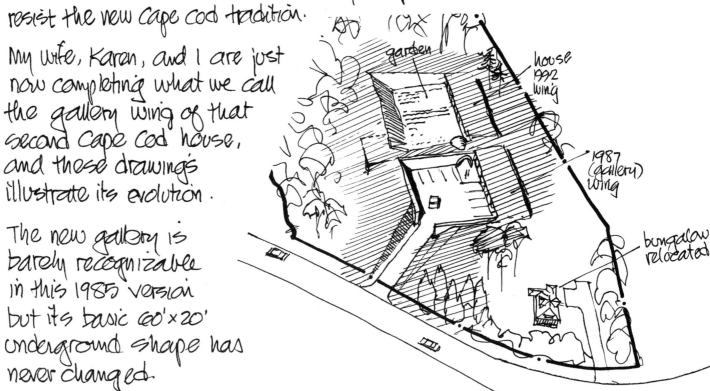

garden

house 1992 wing

1987 (gallery) wing

bungalow relocated

I've long wanted to have a low (5 foot) ceiling area along a north wall in order to allow the rooftop earth to slope down low against the winter winds, and to do away with the high, blank facade usually seen above the small windows on the north sides of buildings, but no, the code won't allow low-head spaces even though they are taken for granted in our cars.

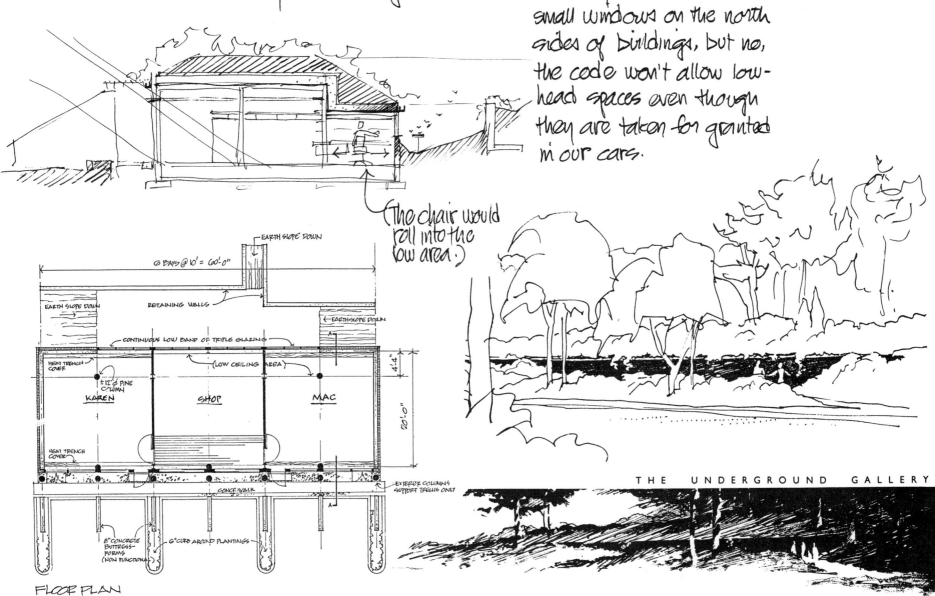

(The chair would roll into the low area.)

EARTH SLOPE DOWN

6 BAYS @ 10' = 60'-0"

EARTH SLOPE DOWN

RETAINING WALLS

←EARTH SLOPE DOWN

CONTINUOUS LOW BAND OF TRIPLE GLAZING

HEAT TRENCH COVER

(LOW CEILING AREA)

4'4"

± 12" Ø PINE COLUMN

KAREN

SHOP

MAC

20'-0"

HEAT TRENCH COVER

EXTERIOR COLUMNS SUPPORT TRELLIS ONLY

CONC. WALK

A

8" CONCRETE BUTTRESS FORMS (NON FUNCTIONAL)

6" CURB AROUND PLANTINGS

FLOOR PLAN
1986

THE UNDERGROUND GALLERY

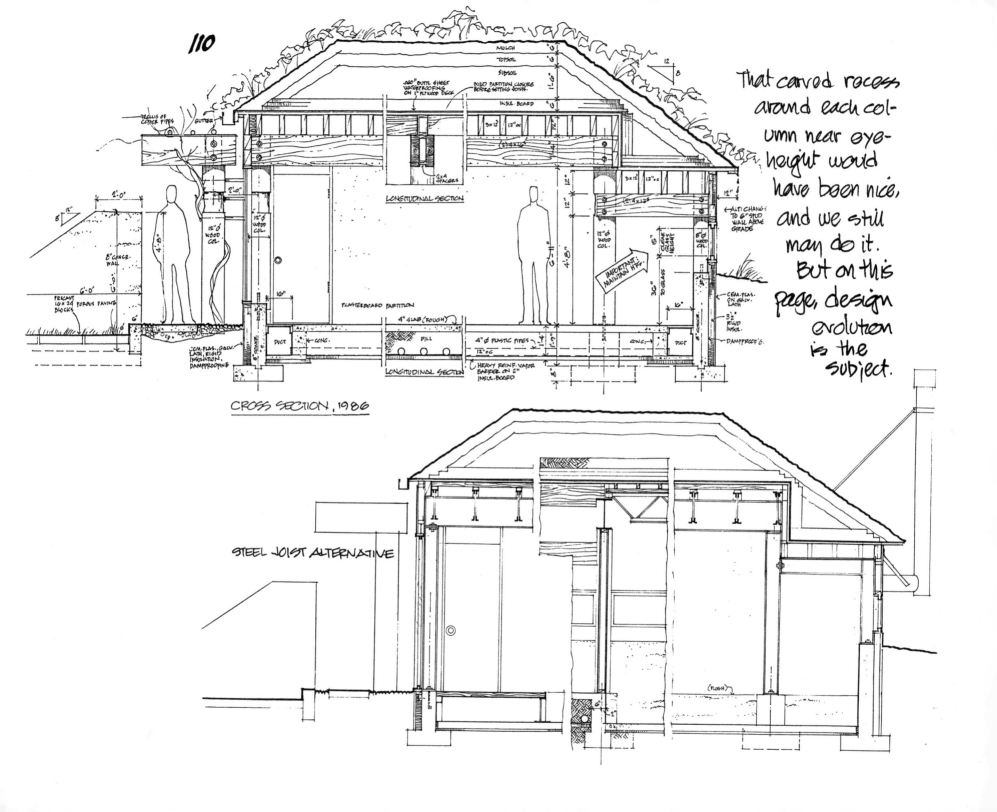

110

That carved recess around each column near eye-height would have been nice, and we still may do it. But on this page, design evolution is the subject.

MULCH
TOPSOIL
SUBSOIL

.060" BUTYL SHEET WATERPROOFING ON 1" PLYWOOD DECK

BUILD PARTITION CLOSURE BEFORE SETTING JOISTS

INSUL. BOARD

3×12    12" OC

(2) 4×16

LONGITUDINAL SECTION

TRELLIS OF COPPER PIPES

GUTTER

3×12    12" OC

(4) 4×12

ALT: CHANGE TO 6" STUD WALL ABOVE GRADE

2×4 SPACERS

2'-0"

2'-0"

12"ø WOOD COL.

12"ø WOOD COL.

12"ø WOOD COL.

12"ø WOOD COL.

6"ø WOOD COL.

8" CONCR. WALL

4'-8"

8" CONCR. WALL

6'-0"

PRECAST 16×24 BLOCKS

POROUS PAVING

CEM. PLAS. GALV. LATH, RIGID INSULATION, DAMPPROOFING

16"

PLASTERBOARD PARTITION

4" SLAB (ROUGH)

DUCT

CONC.

FILL

4" ø PLASTIC PIPES
12" OC

HEAVY REINF. VAPOR BARRIER ON 2" INSUL. BOARD

LONGITUDINAL SECTION

6" SLAB

CROSS SECTION, 1986

IMPORTANT: MAINTAIN HT.

12"

12"

12"

4'-8"

6'-11"

15" CLEAR GLASS HEIGHT

36" TO GLASS

6"

CONC.

DUCT

8" CONCR.

CEM. PLAS. ON GALV. LATH

3½" RIGID INSUL.

DAMPPROOF'G.

1'-9"

STEEL JOIST ALTERNATIVE

(FLUSH)

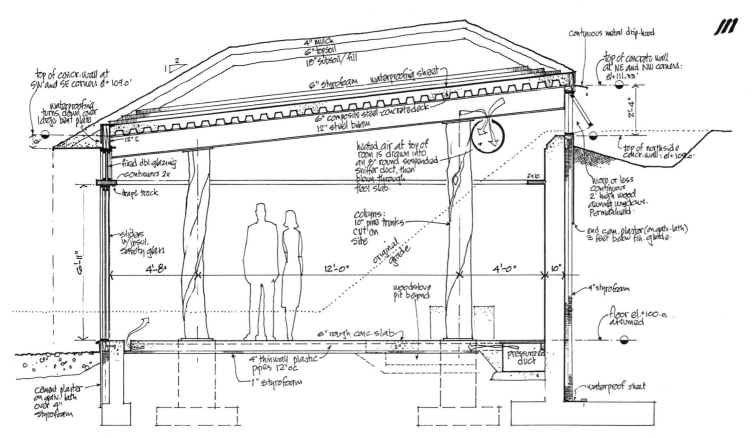

top of concr. wall at SW and SE corners: el + 109.0'

waterproofing turns down over ledge bent plate

fixed dbl glazing — continuous 2x

drape track

sliders w/ insul. safety glass

cement plaster on galv. lath over 4" styrofoam

4" MULCH
6" topsoil
18" subsoil / fill

6" styrofoam    waterproofing sheet

6" composite steel-concrete deck
12" steel beam

12" C

heated air at top of room is drawn into an 8" round suspended sniffer duct, then blown through floor slab.

columns: 10" pine trunks cut on site

original grade

woodstove pit beyond

6" rough conc. slab

4" thinwall plastic pipes 12" oc
1" styrofoam

continuous metal drip-hood

top of concrete wall at NE and NW corners: el + 111.33'

top of northside concr. wall: el + 109.0'

more or less continuous 2' high wood awning windows. Permashield.

end cem. plaster (on galv. lath) 3 feet below fin. grade.

4" styrofoam

floor el. + 100.0, assumed

pressurized duct

waterproof sheet

1  2

2 x 10

6'-11"

4'-8"    12'-0"    4'-0"    10"

These are the as-built <u>section</u>, <u>eaves detail</u>, and <u>floor plan</u>. opening date: as soon as a lot of @!# legal hassles have been resolved.

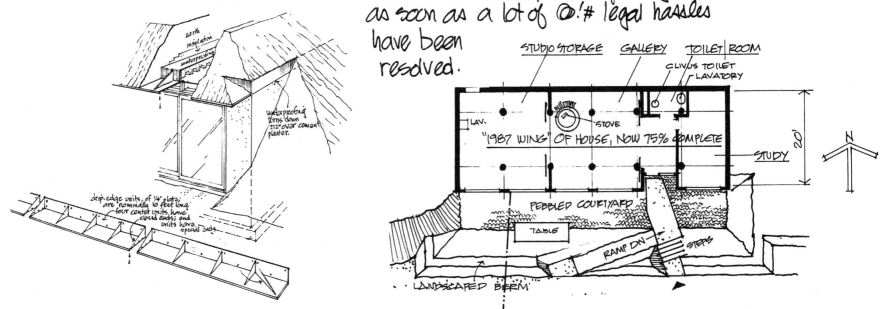

earth insulation
waterproofing
waterproofing turns down ±12" over cement plaster.

drip-edge units, of 1/4" plate, are nominally 10 feet long. four center units have closed ends; end units have special ends.

STUDIO STORAGE    GALLERY    TOILET ROOM
CLIVUS TOILET
LAVATORY

LAV.
STOVE

"1987 WING" OF HOUSE, NOW 75% COMPLETE

STUDY

20'

PEBBLED COURTYARD

TABLE

RAMP DN    STEPS

LANDSCAPED BERM

N

THE UNDERGROUND GALLERY    MW 3·7·88

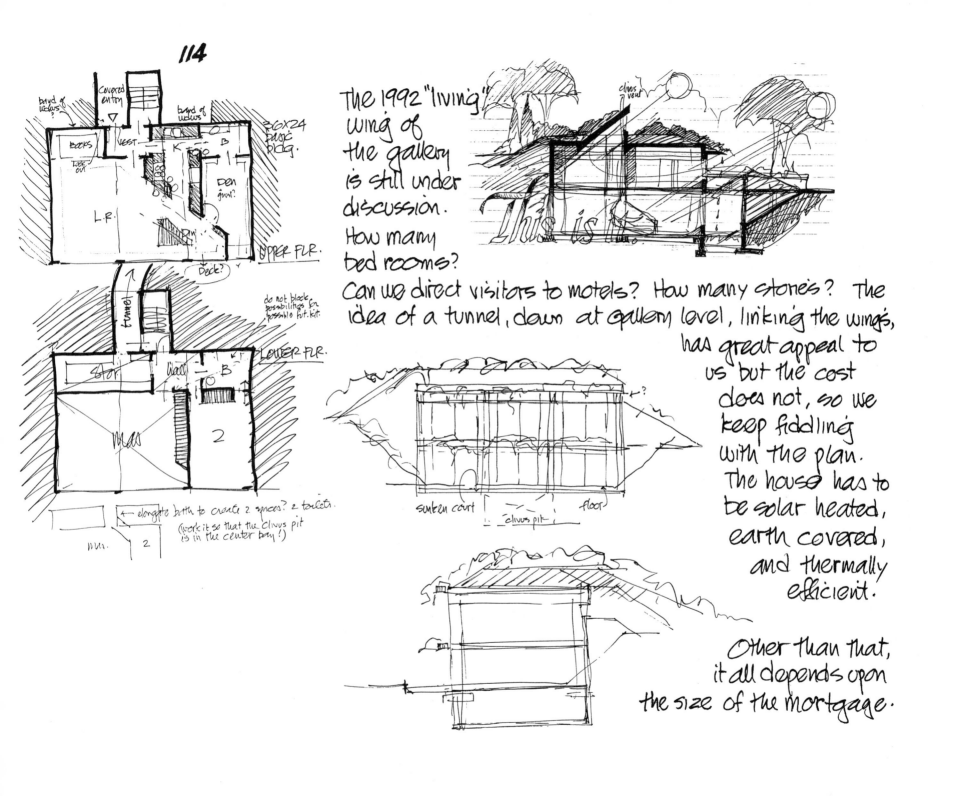

band of windows?

Covered entry

band of windows

36x24 public Bldg.

Books

VEST

look out

K

B

Den guest?

L.R.

UPPER FLR.

Deck?

tunnel

do not block possibilities for possible fut. kit.

LOWER FLR.

Stor

hall

B

man

2

elongate bath to create 2 spaces? 2 toilets. (work it so that the Clivus pit is in the center bay!)

man.

2

The 1992 "living" wing of the gallery is still under discussion. How many bed rooms? Can we direct visitors to motels? How many stones? The idea of a tunnel, down at gallery level, linking the wings, has great appeal to us but the cost does not, so we keep fiddling with the plan. The house has to be solar heated, earth covered, and thermally efficient.

Other than that, it all depends upon the size of the mortgage.

clivus vent

This is

sunken court

clivus pit

floor

What appears at right to be a three-story version of the house is actually four; there has to be an underfloor space for the sewage composter. Too bad. A basement below an underground building, as we proved when building the gallery wing, has to be so heavily reinforced it gets very expensive.

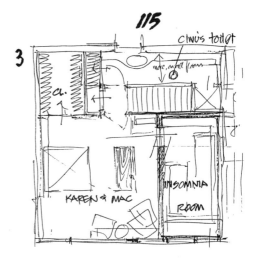

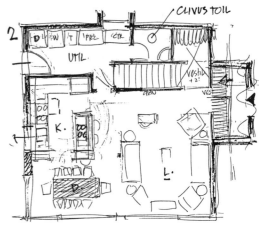

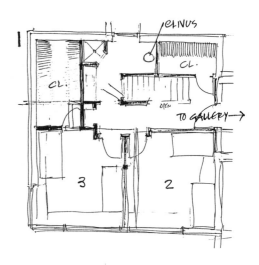

## Waterproofing Underground Buildings

I knew I'd find room for it.

In my almost 20 years of actual construction experience with underground buildings I've never had (knock wood) a wall or roof leak. Skylight leaks, yes. Air leaks around projecting beams, yes, but no underground leaks.* Right from the start, I seem to have stumbled on the right combination and sequence of materials, i.e.—

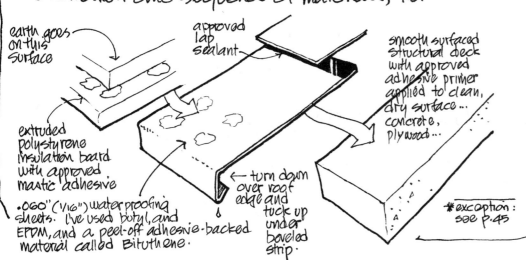

earth goes on this surface

extruded polystyrene insulation board with approved mastic adhesive

.060" (1/16") waterproofing sheets. I've used butyl, and EPDM, and a peel-off adhesive-backed material called Bituthene.

approved lap sealant

← turn down over roof edge and tuck up under beveled strip.

smooth surfaced structural deck with approved adhesive primer applied to clean, dry surface... concrete, plywood...

*exception: see p.45

When a nearby supermarket had stood idle for several months, a local theatre group proposed that it be turned into a neighborhood playhouse. There was talk of attracting theatre crowds from as far away as Boston. 90 miles. Could be.

I couldn't resist offering this tempting earth shelter for the arriving Bostonians. A few days later, the building was rented to an exercise club, and that was that. Good exercise for me, though.

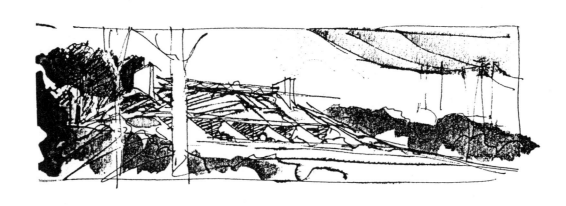

An earth house — to be built near a power line.

And then there was the developer who once let it be known that if Karen and I didn't sign a certain piece of paper he'd build a lot of low-income housing not far from us, thereby presumably lowering the value of our property.

He didn't know he was dealing with a couple of suburban liberals. We thought it sounded like a great idea rather than a threat, and I sent him this design for an earth-covered low-income housing project.

Funny. He never raised the subject again.

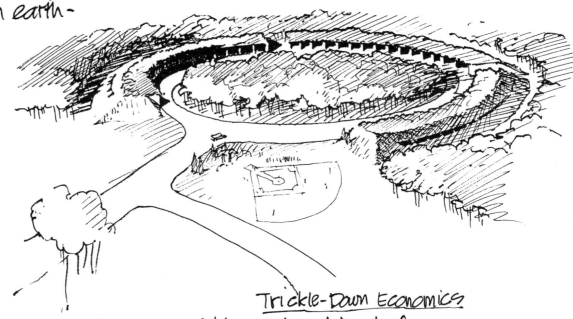

Trickle-Down Economics

It will be a long time before we see low-income housing harvesting the benefits of living in harmony with the land. My clients are usually pretty well off, financially, and my hope is that what they build will benefit less fortunate people by getting all the bugs out of the work.

Kennels are not very popular if they're built near residential areas. Most people, apparently, are like me: cranky about the sound of dogs barking in the night. Or in the daytime, for that matter.

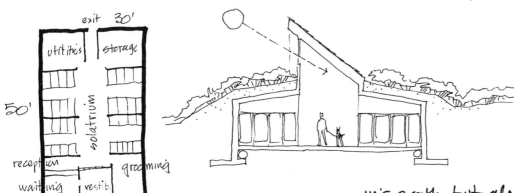

This client wanted — or, I should say, wants, for the project is still on hold — to be a good neighbor. He has picked the most remote part of his site for a kennel, and he plans not only to cover it with sound-deadening earth but also to engage an acoustic engineer to make sure that annoying sounds don't escape through vents or open windows.

I picture a great sun-filled central space and a lot of happy dogs, secure in the knowledge that man has at last come to understand that there is in all canines an atavistic memory of life in dugouts and dens.

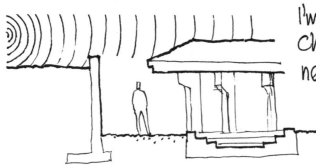

I'm encouraged by memories of my office at Cherry Hill, New Jersey, where the noise of the nearby traffic was somehow lost in the open courtyard set 7' below grade level. It wasn't silent by any means but it was surprisingly quiet.

Not long ago I discovered why they print all those drawings of new and used cars in the back section of the newspaper, after the classifieds and the sports. The drawings are there, apparently, for architects to cut out, or to trace, for use on their building perspectives. The only trouble is the vehicles then look more convincing than the buildings.

A design for John Hait.

A mower Sales & Service Shop in NY state.

ARCHED FACADE CAST IN PLACE ON CURVED FORMS

DRIVEWAY CUT THROUGH HILLSIDE

POROUS PAVING

The majority of American underground houses may very well look like this

but I've seen this one somewhere...in Wisconsin or Minnesota

and in Kansas or Iowa this treated plywood arrangement turned up, with two trees as the only hints of the existence of rooftop earth.

For a while I toyed with the idea of having sun reflectors outside windows in the winter. But the problems...!

Better to stick with what I know will work, and the sniffer duct + underfloor tubes combination works really well on very little electric power.

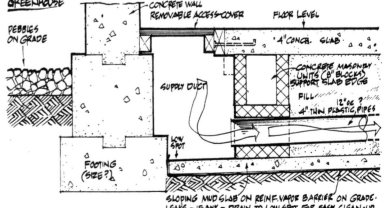

GREENHOUSE

PEBBLES ON GRADE

CONCRETE WALL
REMOVABLE ACCESS COVER   FLOOR LEVEL

4" CONCR. SLAB

SUPPLY DUCT

CONCRETE MASONRY UNITS (8" BLOCKS) SUPPORT SLAB EDGE

FILL

12" O.C. ?
4" THIN PLASTIC PIPES

FOOTING (SIZE?)

LOW SPOT

SLOPING MUD SLAB ON REINF. VAPOR BARRIER ON GRADE.
LEAKS - IF ANY - DRAIN TO LOW SPOT FOR EASY CLEAN-UP.

A related detail appears on p. 137.

John Hait (see p. 48) is the man who knows about using "umbrellas" of insulation in the earth to hold great amounts of warmth in the surrounding soil. Before I read his book I'd heard rumors about the practice, leading me to produce this variation on the umbrella scheme. This scheme misses the best, the warmest place, to store heat: right above the roof. But then that's where the most severe weather exposure occurs. So....?

Structure is insulated on lower surface, and water-proofed (arrow), ready for backfill.

Insulation board (arrow) is applied to carefully-smoothed bank, up to halfway line.

Backfill is placed and tamped around building, insulation board (arrow) is applied to carefully-smoothed slope.

Backfill, topsoil, mulch, and landscaping are added. Earth "inside" insulation stabilizes building temperatures.

reflectors and sun control

·····

plus cross ventilation and more sunlight

·····

with a sniffer duct system added

·····

and multiplied by 200 equals Happy Hill Acres.

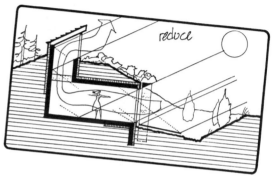

reduce

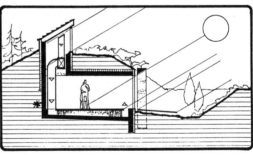

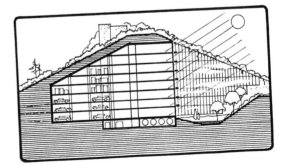

*see that asterisk? Think of all the heat washed away from the wall as rainwater, percolating downward. steals it.

It could be the entrance to a turnpike of the future but it was designed to be the entrance & control point of a big new golf course.

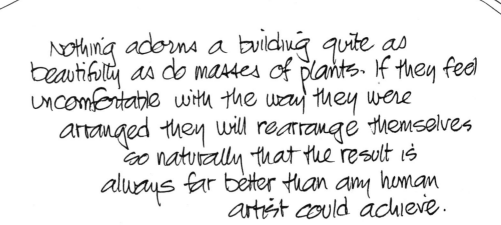

Nothing adorns a building quite as beautifully as do masses of plants. If they feel uncomfortable with the way they were arranged they will rearrange themselves so naturally that the result is always far better than any human artist could achieve.

A little farther in, along a winding drive, a straightaway appears, and there, at the side of it, is the clubhouse itself with its 3 tiers overlooking the course on the other side. I'd be so happy to see a golf club build something like this I'd be almost tempted to try playing a game just to see what it is that people like about hitting a little ball for a mile or so.

This was not a make-believe project. In 1987, I was asked by the club's trustees to submit a design for the clubhouse they hoped to build when all the paperwork had been done to permit construction of this course in Southern New Jersey.

"A very interesting concept," they responded, not quite killing all my hopes.

Well, someday, somewhere, it's bound to happen.

I'm perfectly willing to outwait them, for goodness and truth are on my side. Why don't they recognize that?

This little earthen skywalk is an embellishment taken from some of my correspondence with the club trustees.

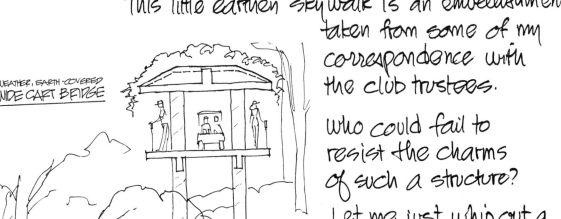

ALL-WEATHER, EARTH-COVERED 12' WIDE CART BRIDGE

Who could fail to resist the charms of such a structure?

Let me just whip out a little structural sketch. Waterproofing sheets can be cut and folded to cover almost any

combination of flat surfaces, especially when complications like pipe penetrations are not involved.

Covered bridges are extremely popular. Think how popular _earth_ covered bridges will be. That's

Why, when I
was asked
to design
this footbridge
into a new
tri-level office
building, I
never thought
twice about
the earth-
covered part.
It's the only
way to go.

(Still "on hold",
this one,
also in New
Jersey.)

NORTH WING

RECESS ENTRANCE WALL UP TO HERE

PLANTED ROOF

SOUTH WING

PLASTER

GLASS

RAIL IS EXTENSION OF MAIN FLOOR SPANDREL

ENTRANCE CIRCLE

BRIGHT FLOWERS →

PLASTER

ENTRANCE STUDY

SLOPING PLANT BED: GROUND COVER AND TREES

FREESTANDING STAIR INSIDE GLASS

PEBBLES

By the year 2050, there will be hardly anyone still alive who remembers when there was even a dispute over whether living plants should be made the central design feature of architecture. For both practical and impractical reasons, it's simply the best way to treat outdoor surfaces on this particular planet.

China! 1985.
An earth-covered, solar,
organic health center in China!

I got so excited when I heard about
the project I could think of little else
for weeks. The cost of the books alone
was more than I'd paid for books in years.
China was my life, and I slowly came
to recognize the names of places that, a few
weeks
earlier, had been utterly unknown
to me. I was going to China!
Money would be forthcoming.
It was all set.

I worked 12, 14 hours
a day on the designs,
making sure the roof-
tops really would dis-
appear as, in the
caption above, I had
said they would.

PLANTED ROOFTOPS (BEYOND) TEND TO DISAPPEAR
WHEN VIEWED FROM PRIVATE PATIO-BALCONY

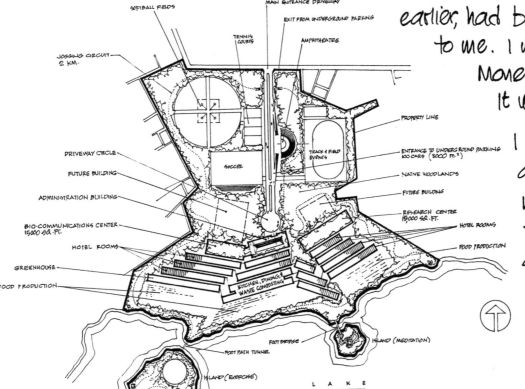

SOFTBALL FIELDS

MAIN ENTRANCE DRIVEWAY

EXIT FROM UNDERGROUND PARKING

TENNIS COURTS

AMPHITHEATRE

JOGGING CIRCUIT 2 KM.

PROPERTY LINE

DRIVEWAY CIRCLE

SOCCER

TRACK & FIELD EVENTS

ENTRANCE TO UNDERGROUND PARKING 100 CARS (3000 m.²)

FUTURE BUILDING

NATIVE WOODLANDS

ADMINISTRATION BUILDING

FUTURE BUILDING

BIO-COMMUNICATIONS CENTER 15,000 SQ. FT.

RESEARCH CENTER 15,000 SQ. FT.

HOTEL ROOMS

HOTEL ROOMS

FOOD PRODUCTION

GREENHOUSE

FOOD PRODUCTION

KITCHEN, DINING, & WASTE COMPOSTING

FOOT BRIDGE

ISLAND (MEDITATION)

FOOT PATH TUNNEL

ISLAND (EXERCISE)

L A K E

But then the client disappeared before the rooftops ever got their chance to do the same.

It's not the unpaid bills that hurt so much. And I'm not at all sure, now, that a suburban U.S. architect should have been involved there. I just don't understand how that slippery guy could have dropped the project without saying a word.

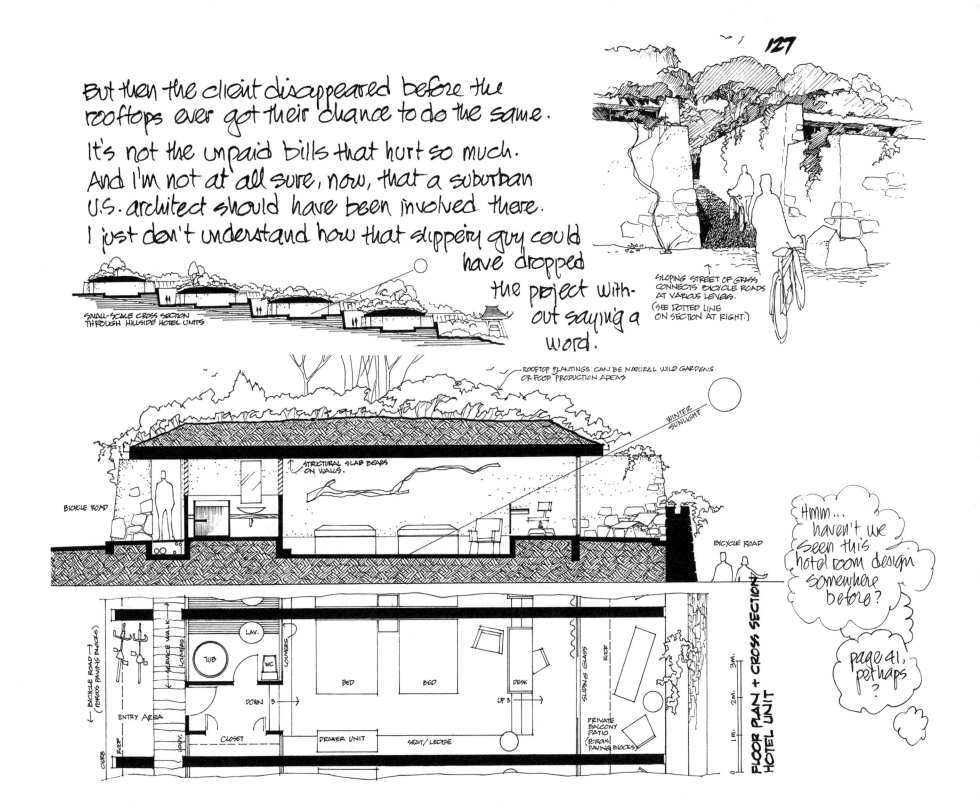

SMALL-SCALE CROSS SECTION THROUGH HILLSIDE HOTEL UNITS

SLOPING STREET OF GRASS CONNECTS BICYCLE ROADS AT VARIOUS LEVELS.
(SEE DOTTED LINE ON SECTION AT RIGHT.)

ROOFTOP PLANTINGS CAN BE NATURAL WILD GARDENS OR FOOD PRODUCTION AREAS

WINTER SUNLIGHT

STRUCTURAL SLAB BEARS ON WALLS.

BICYCLE ROAD

BICYCLE ROAD

Hmm... haven't we seen this hotel room design somewhere before?

page 41, perhaps?

BICYCLE ROAD (POROUS PAVING BLOCKS)

SERVICE WALK

LOUVERS

ROOF

LAV.

TUB

WC

LOUVERS

BED

BED

DESK

UP 3

SLIDING GLASS

ROOF

ENTRY AREA

LOU.

DOWN 3

CLOSET

DRAWER UNIT

SEAT/LEDGE

PRIVATE BALCONY PATIO (POROUS PAVING BLOCKS)

CURB

ROOF

3 M.

2 M.

1 M.

0

FLOOR PLAN + CROSS SECTION HOTEL UNIT

Northwest of Philadelphia, there are places where the last glacier ran
out of steam and left all its debris for someone else to pick up. 10,000
years (or so) later, some clients asked me if it was possible to build
a house on a hillside covered with car-sized, and even garage-sized
rocks. I wasn't sure till I saw them. What I found was a forest of
big old trees growing among, and occasionally on or through, the
boulders.

"Stilts," I said, and "earth cover. Passive solar, too."

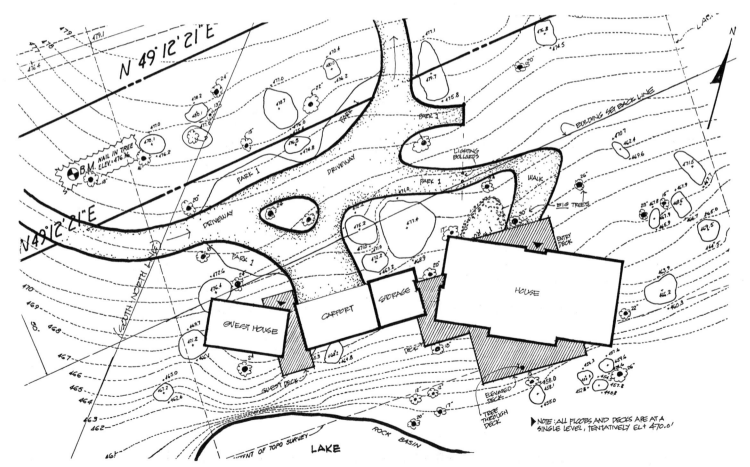

It seemed obvious from the surveyor's information that the house could go in only one place, especially if it was to have a good view of the small lake on the southern edge of the site.

An <u>under-ground</u> house, up in the air, on the rocks, so to speak? It seemed appropriate enough ... until the bids came in. Getting the earth up there by crane on that wooded, bouldered site — and then supporting it — strained the budget just a little too much. The owners were as reluctant as I but the earth had to go, so they built the house with an almost-flat tar-and-gravel roof.

On these pages you'll see the earth covered version for the last time.

GUEST WING    CARPORT    STORAGE    KITCHEN    LIVING    BED ROOM

SOUTH (LAKESIDE) ELEVATION
NOTE SCALE OF HUMAN FIGURES.

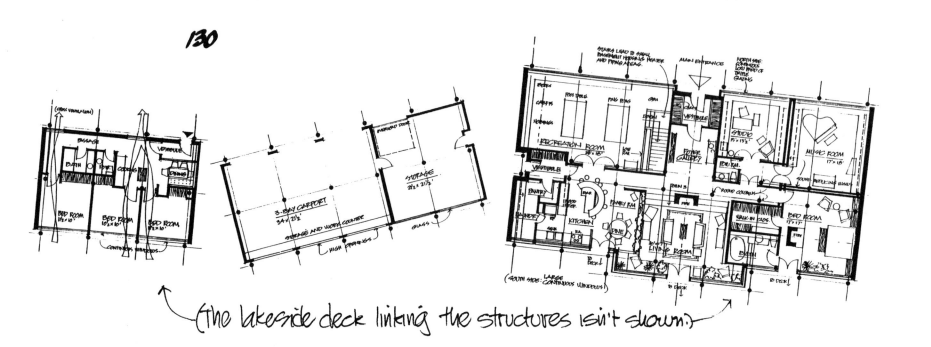

(The lakeside deck linking the structures isn't shown.)

Yes, as usual, and perhaps rightly so, the budget prevailed. The architect selected to do the construction drawings and manage the project managed to save even more money. By putting the guest quarters on top of the carport, and simplifying the plan, he got the figures to come out right so that construction could begin.

I should probably be publishing his version of the design but this is my book, and the subject is underground architecture. The question, in that regard, is: was this a justifiable use of earth cover? Even if the budget had been unlimited, would the greening of these few thousand square feet of roof surface have been defensible in any world-environment sense? I'm too biased to say. The answer has to involve the energy "costs" of placing and carrying all that weight vs. the environmental damage caused by an impervious, lifeless rooftop over the lifetime of the building.

I want to hear what the answer is after, say, 50 years have passed. Our environmental perspective should be in much sharper focus by then.

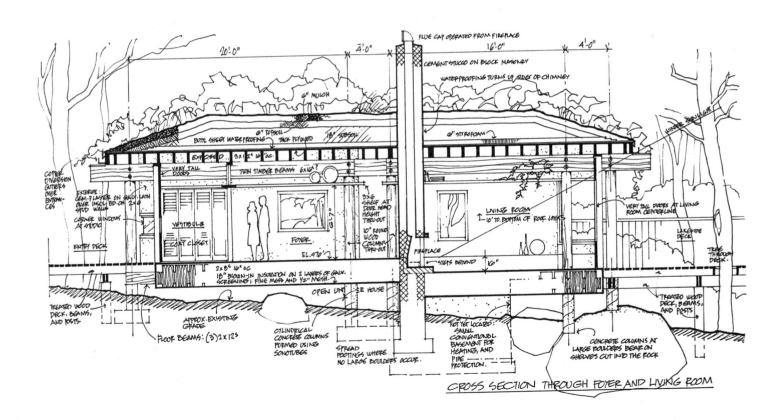

CROSS SECTION THROUGH FOYER AND LIVING ROOM

An airlock entrance vestibule on this north side,
along with small, sit-down-height windows,
helps resist the tendency of hard-won
solar warmth to escape through
to cold side of the house.
Cement plaster over heavily-insulated
walls completes the weather armor.

S.E. Corner

ENTRANCE DESIGN STUDY

The note at the bottom says it all about this interior view, looking toward the southeast.

When wood columns are involved, I'm getting to like round ones more and more, especially when they have the natural roundness of tree trunks.

All those tons of earth weren't to be carried by the bolts alone. The columns were to be notched enough to offer at least partial support directly on their shoulders.

door to bed room

foyer rug

door to rec room

stools

10" wood post

living room

dining

deck

lake

kitchen

If there's confusion as to which are columns and which are trees, well, that's the way it's supposed to be.

Oh, my: there are those 1950s chairs again! And here I am, still not seeing what's wrong with them.

The wood truss house, from the book* my son, Sam, and I did in 1980, is one of my favorites but in

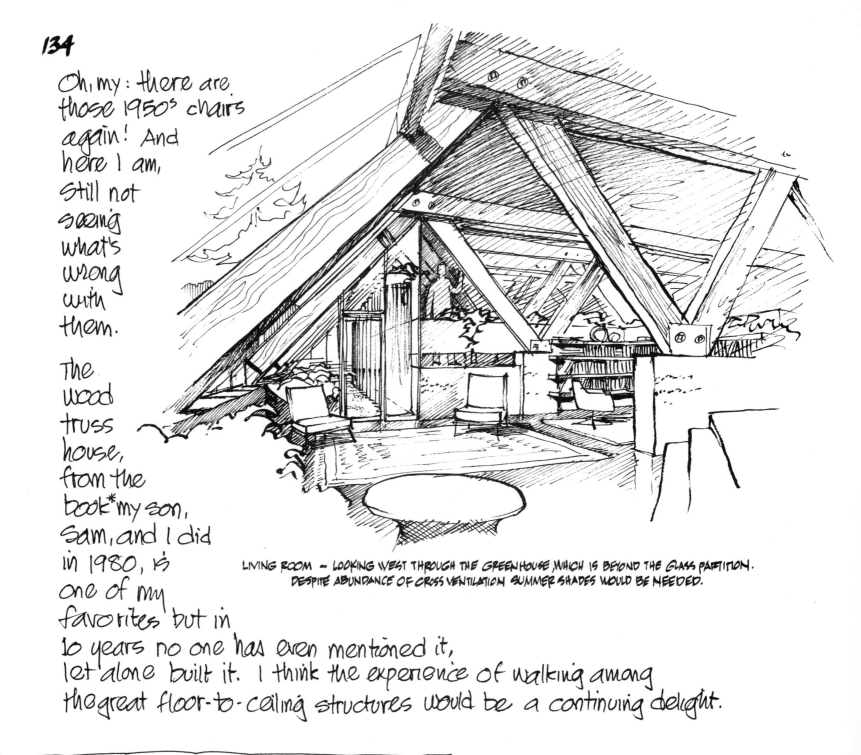

LIVING ROOM — LOOKING WEST THROUGH THE GREENHOUSE, WHICH IS BEYOND THE GLASS PARTITION. DESPITE ABUNDANCE OF CROSS VENTILATION SUMMER SHADES WOULD BE NEEDED.

10 years no one has even mentioned it, let alone built it. I think the experience of walking among the great floor-to-ceiling structures would be a continuing delight.

* Underground Plans Book 1. 1980 $15 postpaid, right here.

Truss house, exterior view.
Rainwater, from the roof-edge gutter, will run down
the hanging chain and step off onto the ground without a splash.
It's an old, old - Colonial or earlier - device I borrowed
for your pleasure.

Another house from the same father-and-son book,
this one aroused just about as much interest as the truss house.

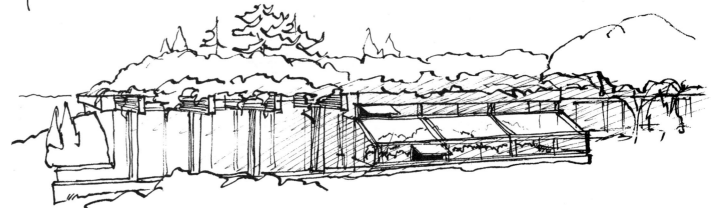

More details from
Underground Plans Book 1,
the book I saw, in the
heat of America's
energy-crisis
infatuation with
solar/earth shelters,
as but the first of a
great series.
Sales were brisk
for a while, and orders
still come along at the
rate of 1 or 2 a month.
Lately, there's even been
a slight and consistent
upturn in sales, and it was
on the basis of that upturn
that I gathered my courage
to publish this book.
With oil prices still relatively
low, I can attribute the recent
upturn to only one thing: an
emerging environmental concern. And that's the best news of the decade.

IF EARTH AT ROOF EDGES IS RAKED BACK TO ITS NATURAL ANGLE OF RE-POSE AND THEN COVERED WITH DEEP MULCH THE BANKS SHOULD NOT ERODE. IN DRYER PARTS OF THE COUNTRY (NOT DESERT AREAS; WE DON'T KNOW WHAT'S BEST THERE) BALED HAY "WALLS" ALONG ROOF EDGES, WEIGHTED WITH ROCKS, AND SURROUNDING LEVEL SOIL BEDS, SHOULD GIVE NATIVE GRASSES AND WILDFLOWERS A CHANCE TO TAKE OVER AND HOLD THE SOIL.

REMEMBER THAT UNWARY PERSONS COULD FALL FROM THE EDGES OF EARTH-COVERED ROOFS. YOU'VE GOT TO FENCE OR IN SOME OTHER WAY DISCOUR-AGE ROOFTOP TRAFFIC. LOW-COST WIRE FENCING, PAINTED A BROWNISH GREEN (OR WHATEVER THE AVERAGE YEAR-ROUND COLOR OF THE LANDSCAPE IS IN YOUR AREA) AND ZIG-ZAGGED AMONG THE ROOFTOP PLANTS, CAN BE BOTH EFFECTIVE AND INCONSPICUOUS.

OPEN SHEDS, FACING SOUTH, FOR THE STORAGE OF LUMBER, FIREWOOD, CEMENT, SAND, FERTILIZERS, MAINTENANCE EQUIPMENT, BOAT, CAR, MULCH... AND PERHAPS FOR AN OPEN-AIR WOODSTOVE OR FIREPLACE — IF THE "SHED" IS NEAR THE GARDEN — FOR CANNING AND SEASONAL COOKING. A WARM SUNNY SHELTER LIKE THIS, EVEN ON A BITTER COLD DAY, CAN BE A GREAT PLACE TO COOK AND SERVE A MEAL — IF YOU'RE DRESSED PROPERLY.

HOW ABOUT A SCREENED PORCH, PERHAPS A DETACHED ONE... ON THE SAME LEVEL, FOR EASY ROLLING OF SERVING CARTS? WHATEVER YOU DO, BE SURE TO LET THE STRUCTURE ECHO THE DESIGN OF YOUR HOUSE. IF THERE ARE NO BUGS WHERE YOU LIVE YOU CAN CALL IT A SUNSHELTER OR A RAINHOUSE.

There's very little, if anything, to add to what these details have to say so I'm going to go have a cup of coffee while you study this page.

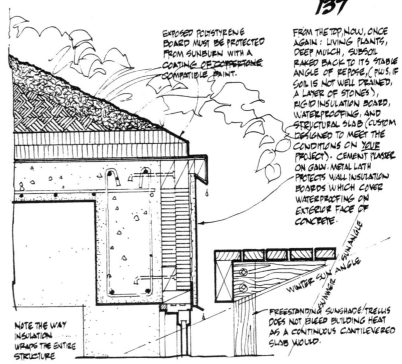

EXPOSED POLYSTYRENE BOARD MUST BE PROTECTED FROM SUNBURN WITH A COATING OF COMPATIBLE PAINT.

FROM THE TOP, NOW, ONCE AGAIN: LIVING PLANTS, DEEP MULCH, SUBSOIL RAKED BACK TO ITS STABLE ANGLE OF REPOSE, (PLUS, IF SOIL IS NOT WELL DRAINED, A LAYER OF STONES), RIGID INSULATION BOARD, WATERPROOFING, AND STRUCTURAL SLAB (CUSTOM DESIGNED TO MEET THE CONDITIONS ON YOUR PROJECT). CEMENT PLASTER ON GALV. METAL LATH PROTECTS WALL INSULATION BOARDS WHICH COVER WATERPROOFING ON EXTERIOR FACE OF CONCRETE.

NOTE THE WAY INSULATION WRAPS THE ENTIRE STRUCTURE

WINTER SUN ANGLE

SUMMER SUN ANGLE

FREESTANDING SUNSHADE/TRELLIS DOES NOT BLEED BUILDING HEAT AS A CONTINUOUS CANTILEVERED SLAB WOULD.

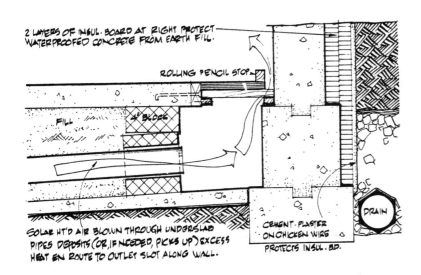

2 LAYERS OF INSUL. BOARD AT RIGHT PROTECT WATERPROOFED CONCRETE FROM EARTH FILL.

ROLLING PENCIL STOP

FILL

4" BLOCK

SOLAR HT'D AIR BLOWN THROUGH UNDERSLAB PIPES DEPOSITS (OR, IF NEEDED, PICKS UP) EXCESS HEAT EN ROUTE TO OUTLET SLOT ALONG WALL.

CEMENT PLASTER ON CHICKEN WIRE PROTECTS INSUL. BD.

DRAIN

(the companion to this detail can be found on page 120.)

In his infinite wisdom, the editor of Popular Science decided to publish this house, called "Low and Bermed," along with another of my design (a house on stilts for construction in low areas), in the June, 1984, issue. Readers were told that if they sent me $63 they would be sent construction plans, details, and specifications for the house they preferred.

If I had plotted the sales, they would have fallen, quite predictably, on a graph something like this: ▨▨▨. What I didn't predict was the length of the tail on that graph. Here I am, six years later, still getting occasional orders for the houses. The latest was an order for the stilt house drawings. It came from Pago-pago!

←This house, however, is the sales leader.

The many uses to which the smaller of the two buildings can be put appears to be responsible for a good deal of the enthusiasm for this design.
Storage room, workshop, hideaway, playroom, the 14' x 12' structure can be modified quite easily for use as a guest house or even a garage.

Steep berms, echoing the slopes of the roofs, offer weather buffering, a landscape theme, and a unifying touch.

Can you identify all the rooms?

The house is 28' x 36'.

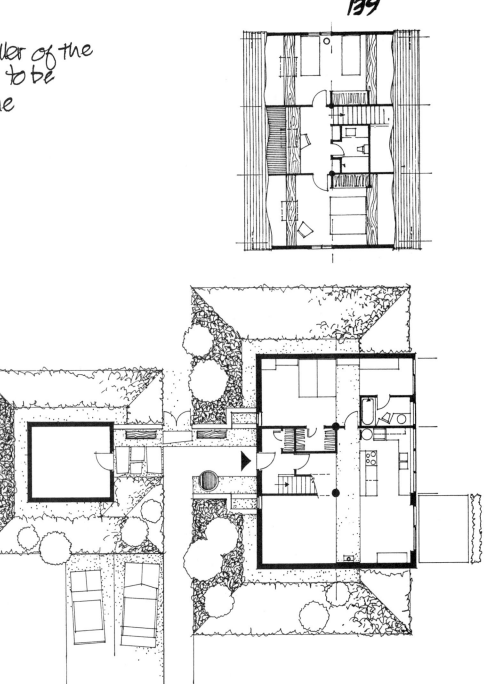

Dogged persistence, isn't that the key? How many times have you seen this pond-at-the-window-sill design so far? Two? Three? I just keep pushing for it, knowing that sooner or later it will get built.

The key to its success, of course, is in having an absolutely fail-safe drain, by gravity, from the "safety overflow and maintenance walk" between the water and the building.

First-time visitors will no doubt be just a little uneasy in a room so obviously below water level but, after a time, the nearness of ducks and boats, of ice or ripples, and of magnificent reflections should be downright addictive.

By holding back the supporting columns, the wall of glass is left nearly unbroken, offering sweeping views of the lake.

LOW-MAINTENANCE NATIVE PLANTS

6" MULCH
6" TOPSOIL
18" SUBSOIL

WATERPROOFING
6" RIGID INSULATION
SLAB

LAKE

POND LEVEL AT SILL (AND DESK) HT.

CARPETED SLAB
RIGID INSULATION

RETAINING WALL
SAFETY OVERFLOW AND MAINTENANCE WALK

Every time I refine this idea I wonder about the surprises that lie locked up in it somewhere, waiting to cause trouble. A tidal wave? Not on a little lake. An earthquake? What damage would it do? A 500-foot oil tanker gone far astray in the fog? The Loch Ness monster? In my experience so far, the few surprises — negative ones — related to earth cover have been far out-weighed by the positive ones. (May it always be so, he wishes with fervor.)

"Send us a proposal," said the fire station's building committee. I did, and illustrated it with my recommendation. They were never heard from again, either. No doubt they'll build another Cape Cod cottage with garage doors across its front. Ah, but what a joy it was to dream this dream of an underground fire station!

Right at the edge of a cranberry bog, the site is certainly one of the most idyllic of American firehouse locations. Seven years have passed so far, with no sign of activity, not even a sign of a construction sign on the site. I go by about once a month on other business, never failing to check for progress there.

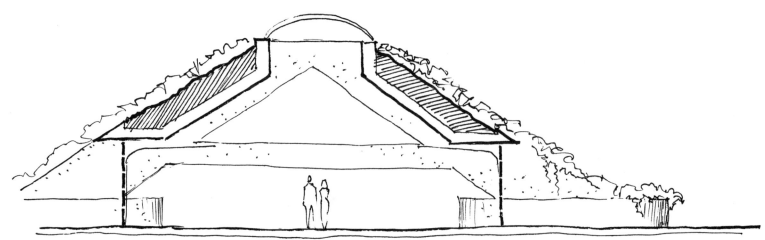

The great skylighted space, the drive-through ease of moving the great engines, the flowering hillsides, and the fireproof construction... even the potential for having offices, storage, and bunk rooms up on a mezzanine level.... how could they resist such an offering?

Only with great courage, I'd say.

If you'll turn the page you'll see even more of the delights so manfully resisted by these Cape Codders.

Earlier, and for another fire house project, I'd done this smaller, double-doored design. Between the doors ran the east-west corridor, fluctuating in temperature because of its single-door protection, but inside the bays a stable and comfortable environment would have been easy to maintain.

JUNE 21

DEC. 21

SCHEMATIC CROSS SECTION @ 1/10" SCALE

NOTE UNDERFLOOR THERMAL MASS, SOLAR HEATING,   CORRIDOR THROUGH AIRLOCK SPACE BETWEEN GLASS OVERHEAD DOORS, NATURAL THROUGH-VENTILATION , AND NATIVE PLANTS.  NATURAL LIGHT. EXTERIOR INSULATION LETS ENTIRE BUILDING STORE HEAT. COOL IN SUMMER WITHOUT CONDENSATION ON WALLS AND FLOOR.

So, which would you rather have, an earth-covered firehouse or a window sill precisely at pond level? It's a tough choice, isn't it?

"First Light", it was to have been called ... a giant theatrical
complex in the forest by the sea, here on Cape Cod ... a place
where the first encounter between Europeans and Native Americans

could be presented, with dignity, drama, and authenticity in an outdoor setting.

The true story was to be told from the Indians' point of view. Historical consultants and some of the actors were to be Cape Cod's Wampanoag Indians. A reproduction Mayflower would sail across the outdoor "stage." The woods themselves would be the backdrop.

Porous paving and an earth-covered roof were to minimize the land damage. Environmental rectitude was to be the design theme. Public interest was aroused, the news media were helpful, and hopes were high. But as site selection difficulties mounted and time began to drag, interest began to drag as well, and the entire project was put on what may be a very permanent kind of hold.

←You can probably tell that I winged that perspective, freehand, without laying out vanishing points. It's probably a little distorted as a result but I think it captures the spirit of the entire design.          R.I.P.

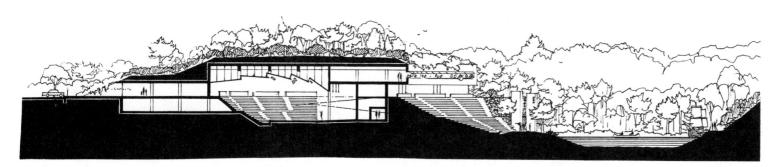

Remember On The Level (p. 52), the book that almost made it to the printer's? This cartoon was to have been a part of it. Shaking the idea that we must impress our neighbors with a facade that has meaning to them is

by no means as easy as it might seem. We — and they — rate conformity right up there with purchase price when it comes to the criteria for selecting a house. We don't admit it, of course, but we all want approval and acceptance, if not outright admiration, from our neighbors.

I couldn't resist putting the Sidwells' name on this drawing because they, of all people, are probably the least concerned about curbside appeal of any couple I know. You must remember their house, back on page 88.

The all-on-one-level book idea came about as a result of requests from all over the country for some designs that would be appropriate in flat land.

One such request came from Richmond. It was a challenge to design a solar/underground house on a vacant lot, 185' x 31', between existing brick houses. The proposed house was to have an insurance office in the basement.

Here's the result.

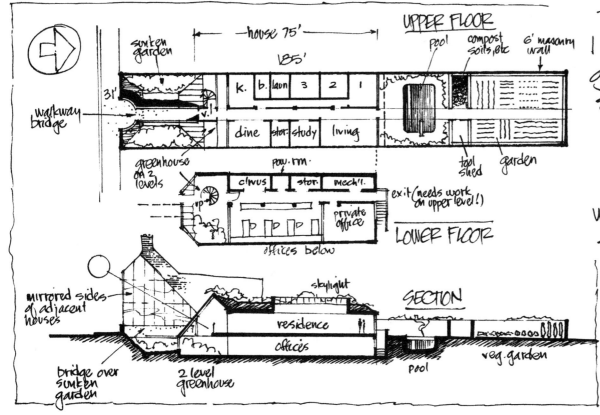

UPPER FLOOR

sunken garden

walkway bridge

house 75'

185'

31'

k. | b. | laun | 3 | 2 | 1

v.

dine | stor. | study | living

greenhouse on 2 levels

pool

compost soils, etc.

6' masonry wall

garden

tool shed

pow. rm.

clivus | stor. | mech'l.

private office

exit (needs work on upper level!)

LOWER FLOOR

offices below

SECTION

mirrored sides of adjacent houses

skylight

residence

offices

bridge over sunken garden

2 level greenhouse

pool

veg. garden

The only way I could see to get adequate sunlight into that slot between the buildings was to mirror the adjoining party walls. Would that have been allowed?

A covered (earth-covered, that is) footbridge from the roadside parking area to the house struck me as the key to this design. The road was on one hilltop, the house on another.

To workshop

A later topographic survey, however, killed the footbridge idea; the actual grades didn't favor it at all, and back to the drawing board I went.

I had to go back a second time when estimates for the construction of the house began to reach well beyond the owners' budget. The original

house (plan, next page) had grown much larger, and the basement workshop (perspective, next page) had been moved into a separate, and not inexpensive, building.

If there are two people on Cape Cod who can match the tolerance and good humor of my Raven Rocks friends in Ohio, it is this couple, Gail Turner and Peter Spier, who, unable to build their expensive dream house, asked me

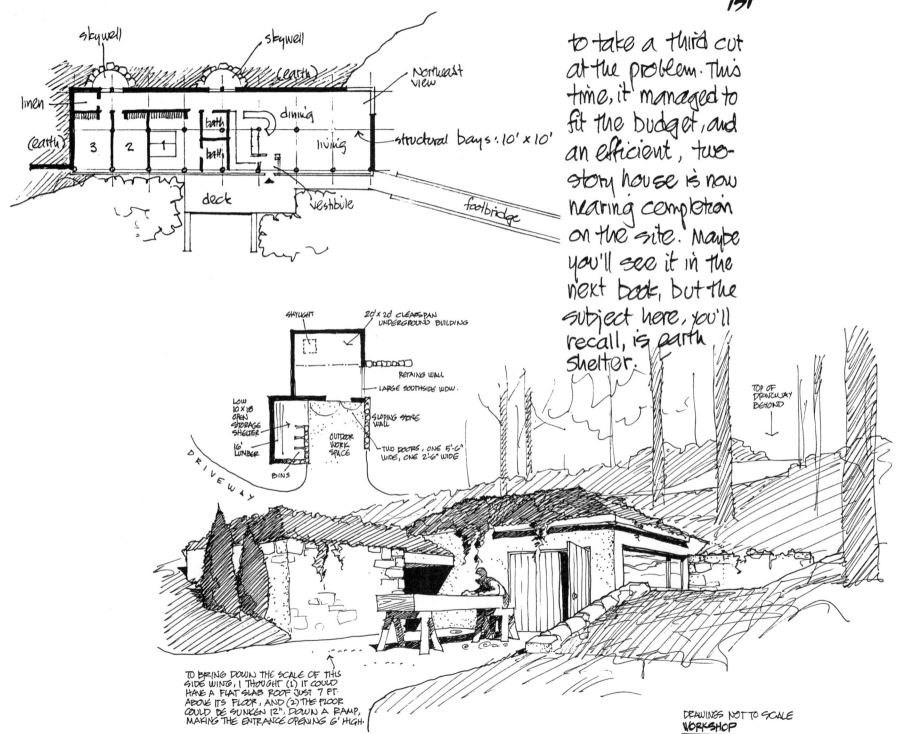

skywell    skywell    (earth)    Northeast view

linen

(earth)    3    2    1    bath    dining    structural bays: 10' x 10'
                        bath    living

deck    vestibule    footbridge

to take a third cut at the problem. This time, it managed to fit the budget, and an efficient, two-story house is now nearing completion on the site. Maybe you'll see it in the next book, but the subject here, you'll recall, is earth shelter.

SKYLIGHT    20' x 20' CLEARSPAN UNDERGROUND BUILDING

RETAING WALL

LARGE SOUTHSIDE WDW.

LOW 10 x 18 OPEN STORAGE SHELTER

SLOPING STONE WALL

16' LUMBER    OUTDOOR WORK SPACE

TWO DOORS, ONE 5'-6" WIDE, ONE 2'-6" WIDE

DRIVEWAY

BINS

TOP OF DRIVEWAY BEYOND

TO BRING DOWN THE SCALE OF THIS SIDE WING, I THOUGHT (1) IT COULD HAVE A FLAT SLAB ROOF JUST 7 FT. ABOVE ITS FLOOR, AND (2) THE FLOOR COULD BE SUNKEN 12", DOWN A RAMP, MAKING THE ENTRANCE OPENING 6' HIGH.

DRAWINGS NOT TO SCALE
**WORKSHOP**

I like to walk an owner through the design process. This stroll was taken with a good-humored school-master who had a dream of getting out of town into the lovely Indiana countryside.

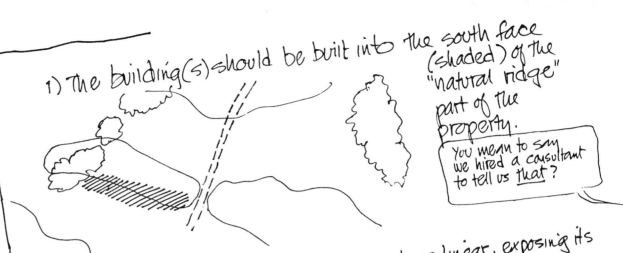

1) The building(s) should be built into the south face (shaded) of the "natural ridge" part of the property.

You mean to say we hired a consultant to tell us _that_?

2) The building(s) should be more or less linear, exposing its long face to the south.

3) A straight rectangular box would be appalling.

4) A free-form shape would be too expensive.

5) A rectangular (90°) plan theme would be least expensive among the irregular-plan choices but it would probably lose too much winter sun-light by casting shadows on itself much of the day.

6) The collision of two rectangular geometries is probably the next best bet in terms of economics.

(Maybe even flatter than that; like this:  )

7) Most classrooms should be on the south side. This means single-loaded corridors.

8) It also means mostly earth-covered corridors, but corridors must not be dark, airless, electrically-lighted tunnels, so...

9) Corridors must do two things:
a) Have high windows, where possible, and
b) Poke out into daylighted sunken gardens at the ends of long runs.

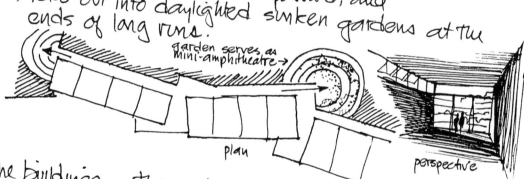

garden serves as mini-amphitheatre →

plan

perspective

10) The buildings— the architecture— must at a glance express the idea of land husbandry, not land domination. Just as contour plowing expresses this in agriculture so does contour architecture in construction. A jumbled series of earth shelters would broadcast confused messages. But you want varied floor levels and different ceiling heights. So do I. Such considerations, to me, lead to one conclusion: a powerful

He liked what he saw of these designs but a misunderstanding as to who was to pay for them got in the way and upset that delicate balance of trust so important to the launching of projects.

(more) →

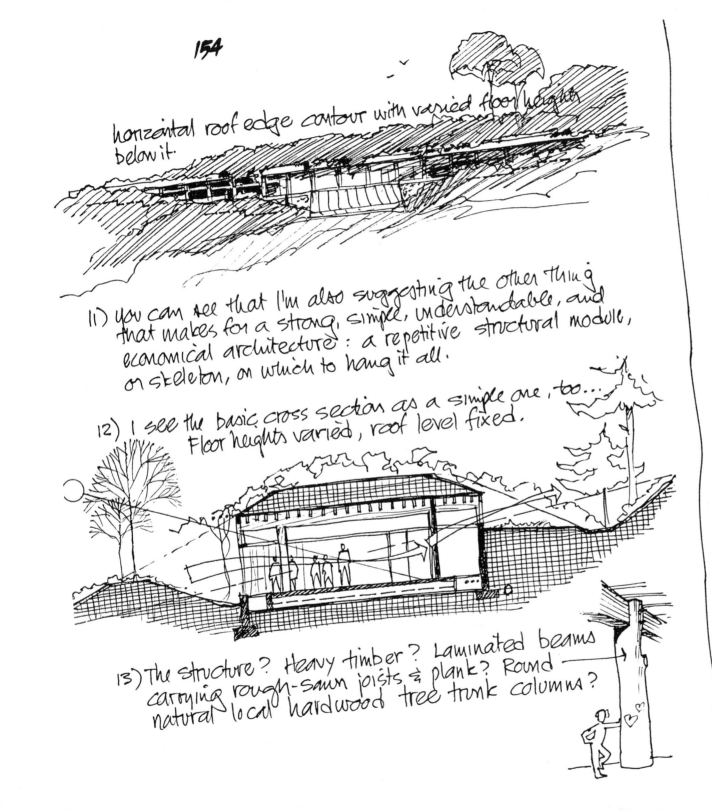

horizontal roof edge contour with varied floor heights below it.

11) you can see that I'm also suggesting the other thing that makes for a strong, simple, understandable, and economical architecture: a repetitive structural module, or skeleton, on which to hang it all.

are you reading all this?

12) I see the basic cross section as a simple one, too...
Floor heights varied, roof level fixed.

13) The structure? Heavy timber? Laminated beams carrying rough-sawn joists & plank? Round natural local hardwood tree trunk columns?

14) And what about having some great, roughly rectangular slabs of your limestone standing inside some of the south-facing glass, to absorb solar energy and to reradiate it, stabilizing interior temperatures?

15) The best I've been able to do, with regard to an actual floor plan, so far, is this:

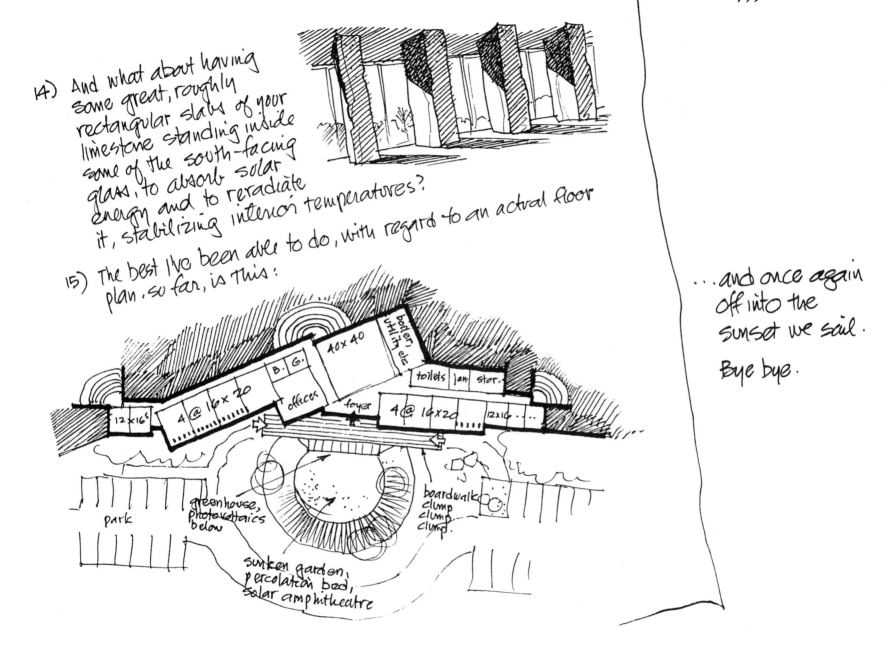

boiler, utility etc

40 × 40

B. G.

offices

12 × 16's

4 @ 16 × 20

foyer

toilets    jan.    stor.

4 @ 16 × 20    12 × 16 . . .

park

greenhouse,
photovoltaics
below

sunken garden,
percolation bed,
solar amphitheatre

boardwalk
clump
clump
clump.

...and once again off into the sunset we sail.

Bye bye.

Another day, another school, this one World College West, the still-struggling little school in Marin County, north of San Francisco. Stressing environmental studies and international affairs, it seems to have just the right recipe for our times.

Founded by my longtime friend, Dick Gray, the college has managed to get itself accredited, to outgrow its original rented army barracks, to acquire a big hilltop campus, and to get some new buildings built. This, I'm afraid, is not one of them.

I was lucky enough to have been involved in the design discussions but my suggestions, as by now you can imagine without being told, were too expensive for the fledgling institution.

Above, a dormitory and amphitheatre. At left, an administration building.

You see no cars in the drawings because the parking lot is down at the foot of the great sprawling hill, near the highway. Only service vehicles and a student shuttle bus make the climb to the campus. The first time I made the climb I was so winded I thought I was a goner. After my heart stopped thudding I realized I'd better get more exercise, and I've been a runner* ever since. So you can see I got an education at the College.

_____

* a mile or so, at a 9-minute rate, every other day, if you can call that running.

Before my first visit to Cape Cod
I thought it was a sand spit
so low it was probably washed
over by the sea during spring tides.
The forest was my first surprise, the
hills were the next. None are
higher than about 100 feet but they
can be quite steep, as the contours at
right indicate, in spite of the mostly
sandy soil.

Only with the permission of the local
Conservation Commission can you
disturb anything within 100 feet (dotted
line) of ponds or wetlands. All of
this proposal except the

87.7

90.8

97.8

88.9

ASSUMED EL
+100.0 TOP
OF ELEC.BOX

N

98   99   100      101      102

90

80

70

60

POND EL: + 54.8'

existing
grade

garden
wall
beyond

patio

driveway
slot
through
embankment

garage
beyond

hedge at veg. garden

entrance
area

bridge

hillside
path

CROSS SECTION ON BUILDING CENTERLINE, LOOKING EAST

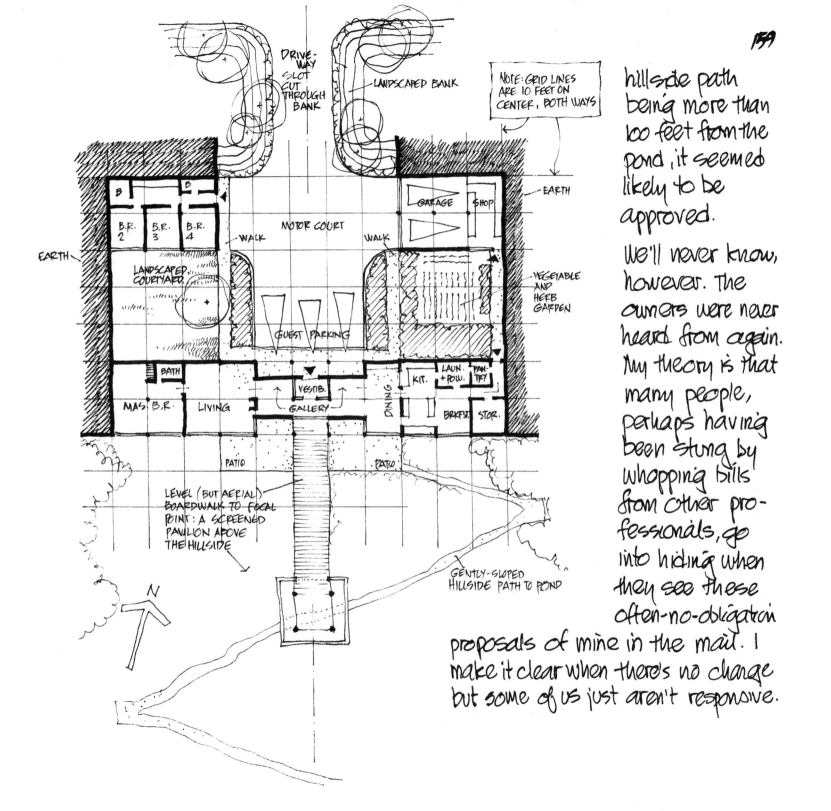

DRIVE-
WAY
SLOT
CUT
THROUGH
BANK

LANDSCAPED BANK

NOTE: GRID LINES
ARE 10 FEET ON
CENTER, BOTH WAYS

EARTH

B          B

B.R.     B.R.     B.R.
2         3        4

EARTH

MOTOR COURT

GARAGE     SHOP

WALK          WALK

LANDSCAPED
COURTYARD

VEGETABLE
AND
HERB
GARDEN

GUEST PARKING

BATH

LAUN.
+ POW.

PAN-
TRY

KIT.

VESTIB.

MAS. B.R.     LIVING          GALLERY

DINING

BRKFST.     STOR.

PATIO                    PATIO

LEVEL (BUT AERIAL)
BOARDWALK TO FOCAL
POINT: A SCREENED
PAVILION ABOVE
THE HILLSIDE

GENTLY-SLOPED
HILLSIDE PATH TO POND

N

hillside path being more than 100 feet from the pond, it seemed likely to be approved.

We'll never know, however. The owners were never heard from again. My theory is that many people, perhaps having been stung by whopping bills from other professionals, go into hiding when they see these often-no-obligation proposals of mine in the mail. I make it clear when there's no charge but some of us just aren't responsive.

Excuse me, but isn't this where we came in?

Could be. It is getting to look awfully familiar, isn't it? But if you are to be convinced of the need for a new gentle architecture you have to become so mesmerized by it that the idea of building into the earth never seems foreign to you again.

The key words: silent, bright, dry, permanent, safe, ever-changing, and potentially beautiful.

Got it?

This potential client did remember to say thank you, and then some, even though nothing ever came of the proposal. Badly-needed low-income housing for the town of Orleans, here on Cape Cod, it simply ran into too many bureaucratic snags.

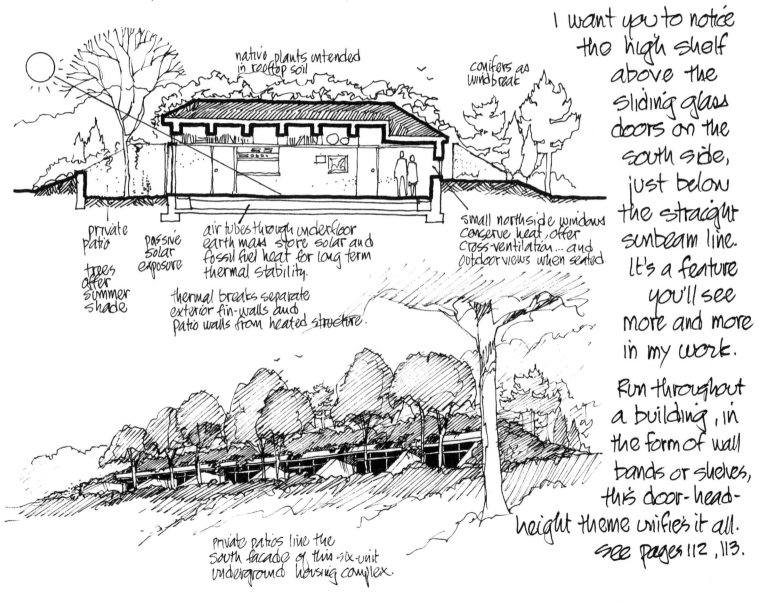

native plants intended in rooftop soil

conifers as windbreak

private patio

passive solar exposure

trees offer summer shade

air tubes through underfloor earth mass store solar and fossil fuel heat for long term thermal stability.

thermal breaks separate exterior fin-walls and patio walls from heated structure.

small northside windows conserve heat, offer cross-ventilation... and outdoor views when seated

private patios line the south facade of this six-unit underground housing complex.

I want you to notice the high shelf above the sliding glass doors on the south side, just below the straight sunbeam line. It's a feature you'll see more and more in my work.

Run throughout a building, in the form of wall bands or shelves, this door-head-height theme unifies it all. see pages 112, 113.

Department of miscellany; another of those future cities with interchangeable, plug-in room-parts beneath permanent earth shelves; underground towers inspired by the purity of stacked porous paving blocks; and another entrance to something or other...

...and here: a Japanese/Cape Cod/Wrightian earth shelter, followed by solar village pyramids, the last bits of straight-line architecture before we go off into a rather extended period of circular designs.

HOUSE : PICTURE FOR JOHN, BOBBIE, & CO.

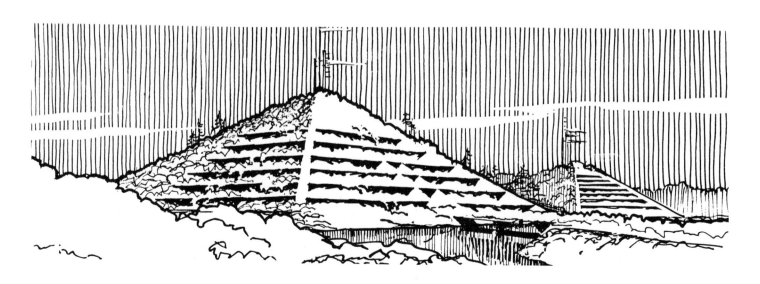

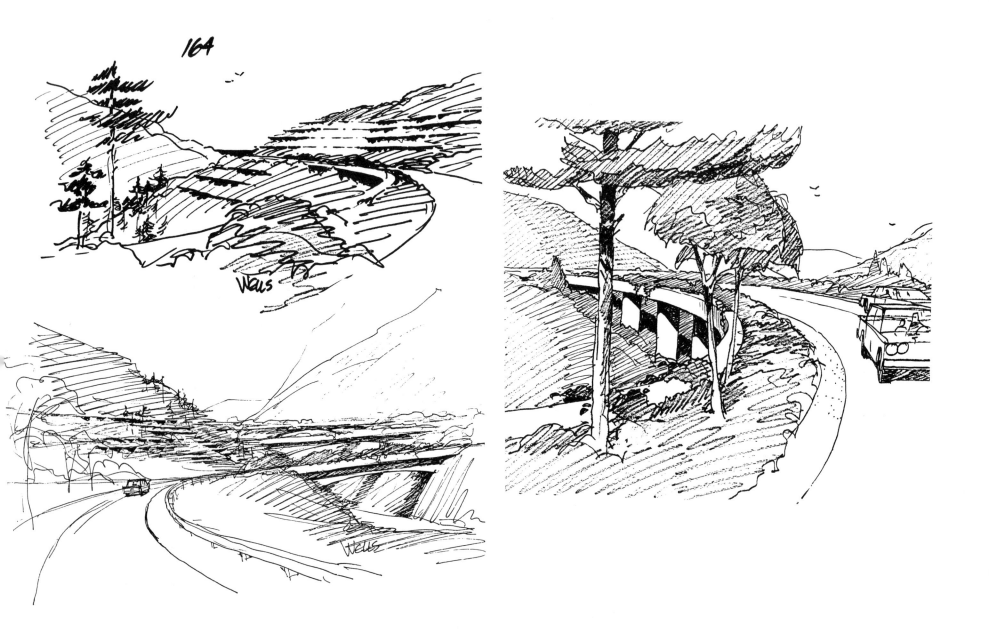

Cherry Hill, New Jersey, 1984. I was sure the developer who called on me for new design ideas for townhouses would be ripe for this idea. It shows what I know about the ripeness of people, particularly developers.

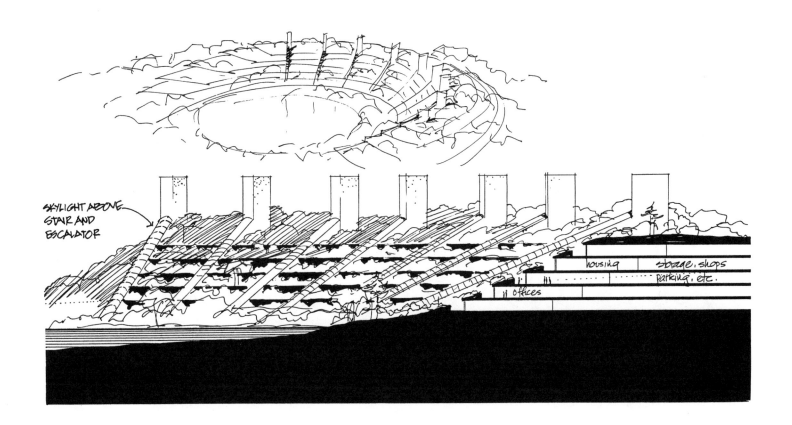

SKYLIGHT ABOVE STAIR AND ESCALATOR

housing    storage, shops

offices    parking, etc.

It's very flattening to be called all the way across America, out to the hills of Los Angeles, to visit the site of a proposed house. It beats a warm shower and a backrub,

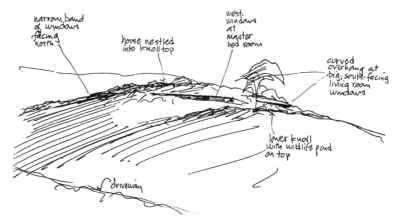

narrow band of windows facing north

house nestled into knolltop

west windows at master bedroom

curved overhang at big, south-facing living room windows

lower knoll with wildlife pond on top

driveway

especially if the site is an entire hilltop, way out in the country, covered with acres of orange poppies.

I spent a long weekend in the area, walking the site, scribbling notes, and talking with the owners. The longer I looked at that round hill the rounder my ideas became until out burst this ring of rooms nestled so low into the crest as to seem a part of it.

Farther up the hill, the owners wanted a small workshop building (p.171). You can just catch a glimpse of it at left.

No, this one never got built, either. The owners suffered some sort of financial

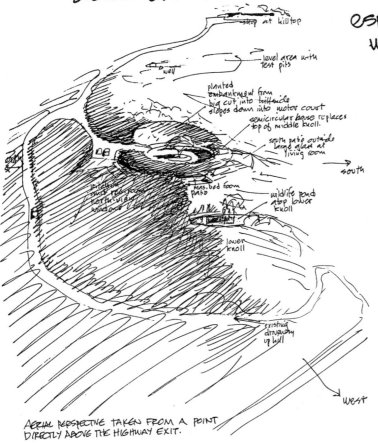

shop at hilltop

level area with test pits

well

planted embankment from big cut into hillside slopes down into motor court

semicircular house replaces top of middle knoll

south patio outside large glass at living room

south

kitchen & mud room with view windows

mas. bed room patio

wildlife pond atop lower knoll

lower knoll

existing driveway up hill

west

AERIAL PERSPECTIVE TAKEN FROM A POINT DIRECTLY ABOVE THE HIGHWAY EXIT.

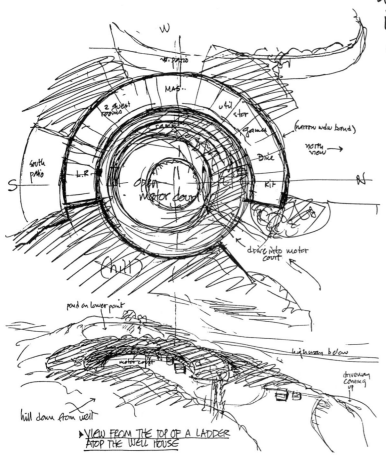

south patio
L.R
S
open motor court
2 guest rooms
util
stor
games
Dine
(narrow wdw band)
north view
N
Kit
drive into motor court

pond on lower point
highway below
motor court
driveway coming up
hill down from well

▶ VIEW FROM THE TOP OF A LADDER ATOP THE WELL HOUSE

setback and had to give it up. While it lasted, our relationship was delightful, full of good idea-exchanges and open-mindedness.

I think I'll let you wander through the house by yourself for a while, and I'll meet you when you get up to the workshop.

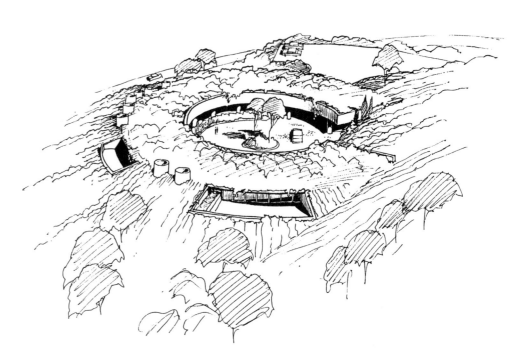

S.W. side.

North is off to the right, south to the left.
The hill continues to climb from this rounded crest eastward (toward the bottom of the page).

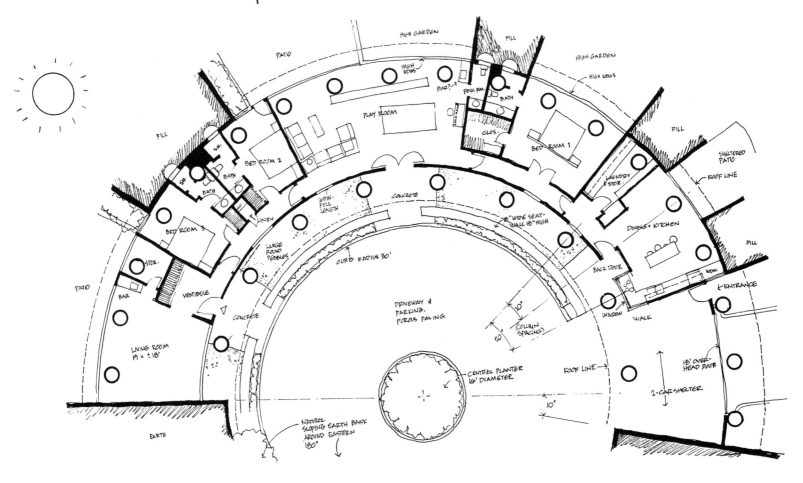

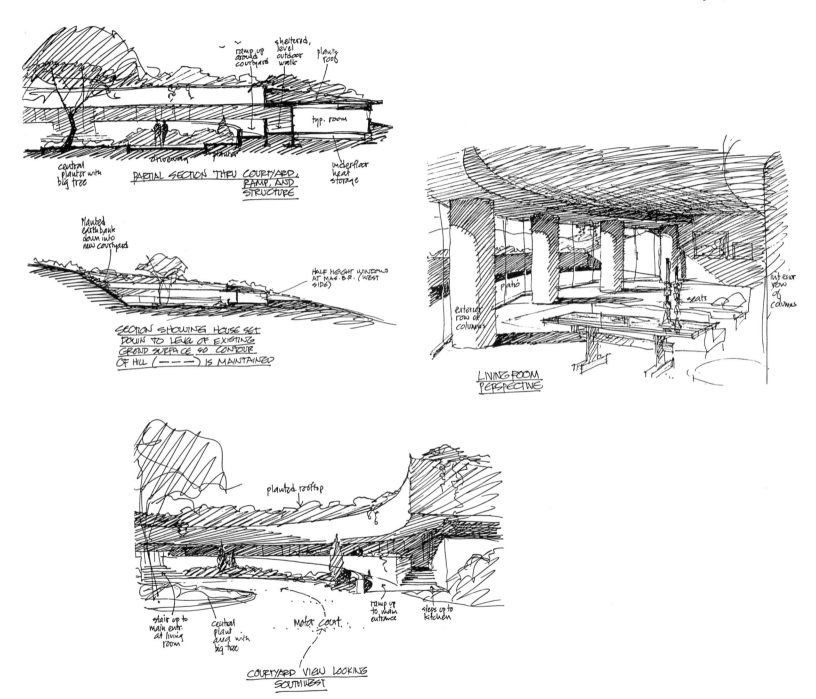

ramp up around courtyard

sheltered, level outdoor walk

planty roof

typ. room

central planter with big tree

driveway

planter

PARTIAL SECTION THRU COURTYARD, RAMP, AND STRUCTURE

underfloor heat storage

planted earth bank down into new courtyards

half height windows at mas. b.r. (west side)

SECTION SHOWING HOUSE SET DOWN TO LEVEL OF EXISTING GROUND SURFACE SO CONTOUR OF HILL (———) IS MAINTAINED

exterior row of columns

patio

seats

interior row of columns

LIVING ROOM PERSPECTIVE

planted rooftop

stair up to main entr. at living room

central plant area with big tree

Motor Court.

ramp up to main entrance

steps up to kitchen

COURTYARD VIEW LOOKING SOUTHWEST

The lower knoll, or crest, obscures part of the freeway (below), and the hill climbs on up toward us as we look down from up near the workshop.
↓

↑ Arriving at the east side. Freeway in the distance, to the West.

The workshop is straight because long, straight things were to be made in it, and because the hillside was straight at that point. The southside solar area can be seen off to the right in this view looking from the west.

Next: two more circular designs before we get back into straight lines again.

A geodesic dome and a 4-level underground building encircling a pond, right in the heart of the city. If all the new buildings downtown were required to put life values first, the wildlife would stage a dramatic comeback.

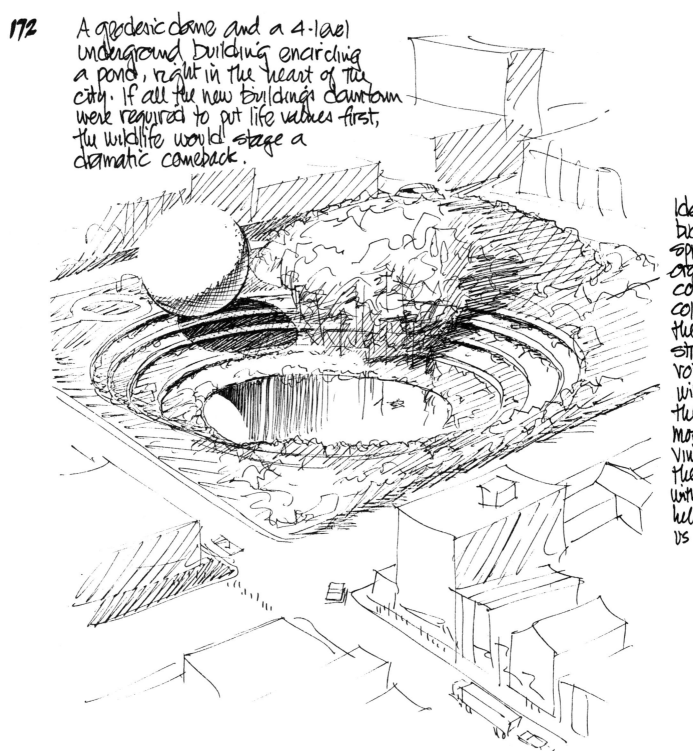

Ideal landscape budget: $ zero. Spread composted organic wastes, cover with leaves collected from the autumn streets, and voila! First: wildflowers, then shrubs, mosses, and vines, and then trees... without any help from us at all.

I was invited to teach an environmental course at Harvard in '83-84. Eight students signed up, and I soon found that they knew a lot more about everything than I did. After spending all those years in high school, undergraduate school, and graduate school they'd become a different species of animal to me.

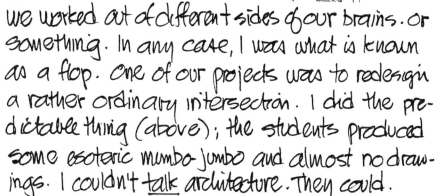

washington st., north

BROOKLINE CIRCLE / Aerial from the south

(all paving within 500' of circle: porous)

- solar / hyacinth sewage ponds
- photovoltaics
- community greenhouse
- underground parking
- all-weather shopping
- food production
- total reforestation
- porous paving
- superinsulation
- wildlife habitat
- edible landscape
- waste mgt.
- percolation

POSITIVELY NO FOTOS!

We worked out of different sides of our brains. or something. In any case, I was what is known as a flop. One of our projects was to redesign a rather ordinary intersection. I did the predictable thing (above); the students produced some esoteric mumbo-jumbo and almost no drawings. I couldn't talk architecture. They could.

At one point we almost organized a summer tour of underground buildings in Sweden.

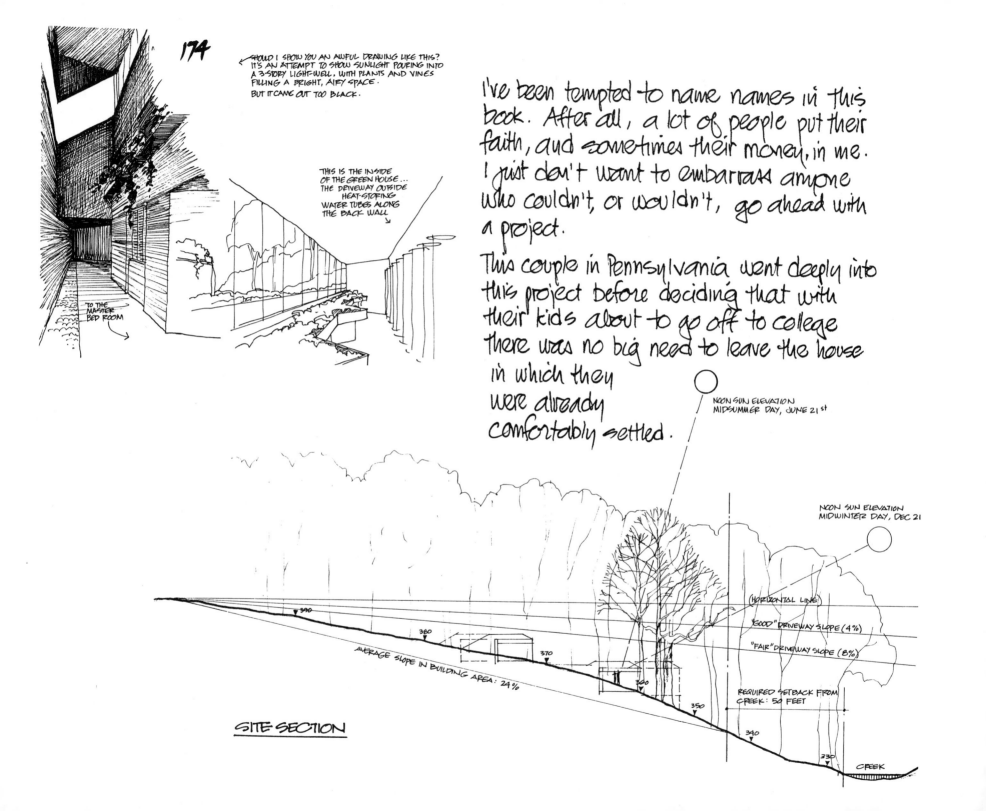

SHOULD I SHOW YOU AN AWFUL DRAWING LIKE THIS?
IT'S AN ATTEMPT TO SHOW SUNLIGHT POURING INTO
A 3-STORY LIGHT-WELL, WITH PLANTS AND VINES
FILLING A BRIGHT, AIRY SPACE.
BUT IT CAME OUT TOO BLACK.

THIS IS THE INSIDE
OF THE GREEN HOUSE...
THE DRIVEWAY OUTSIDE
HEAT-STORING
WATER TUBES ALONG
THE BACK WALL

TO THE
MASTER
BED ROOM

I've been tempted to name names in this book. After all, a lot of people put their faith, and sometimes their money, in me. I just don't want to embarrass anyone who couldn't, or wouldn't, go ahead with a project.

This couple in Pennsylvania went deeply into this project before deciding that with their kids about to go off to college there was no big need to leave the house in which they were already comfortably settled.

NOON SUN ELEVATION
MIDSUMMER DAY, JUNE 21st

NOON SUN ELEVATION
MIDWINTER DAY, DEC 21

(HORIZONTAL LINE)

"GOOD" DRIVEWAY SLOPE (4%)

"FAIR" DRIVEWAY SLOPE (8%)

AVERAGE SLOPE IN BUILDING AREA: 24%

390
380
370
360
350
340
330

REQUIRED SETBACK FROM
CREEK: 50 FEET

CREEK

SITE SECTION

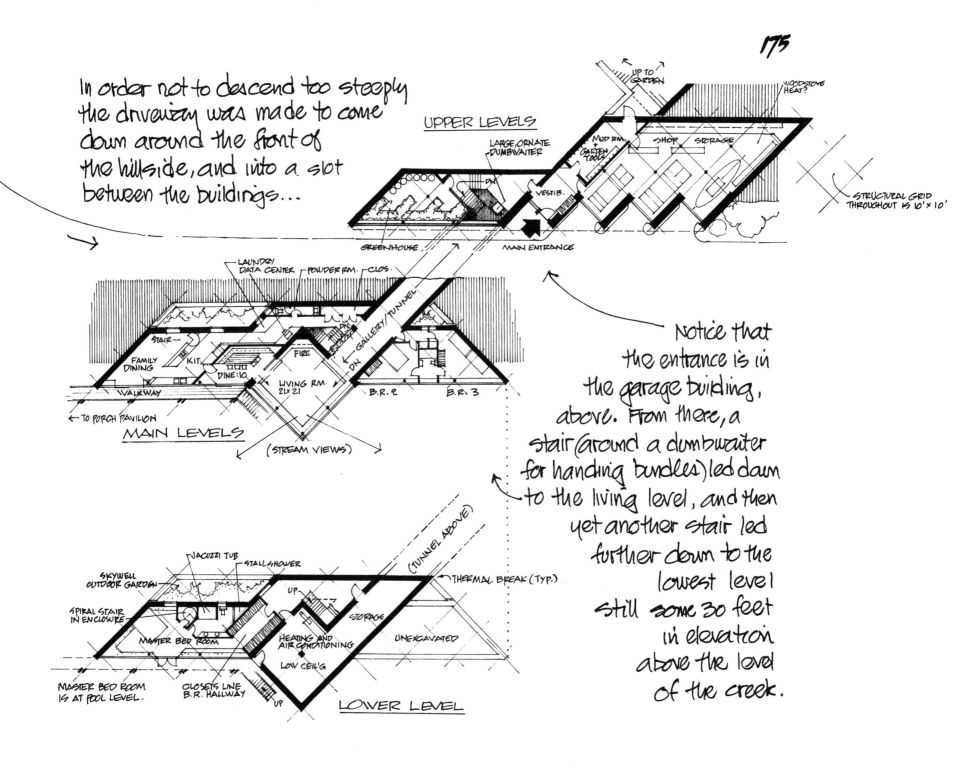

In order not to descend too steeply the driveway was made to come down around the front of the hillside, and into a slot between the buildings...

UPPER LEVELS

UP TO GARDEN

WOODSTOVE HEAT?

LARGE, ORNATE DUMBWAITER

MUD RM. + GARDEN TOOLS

SHOP

STORAGE

DN

VESTIB.

STRUCTURAL GRID THROUGHOUT IS 10'x10'

GREENHOUSE

MAIN ENTRANCE

LAUNDRY DATA CENTER

POWDER RM.

CLOS.

STAIR

DN

DN

GALLERY/TUNNEL

FAMILY DINING

KIT.

FIRE

DINE:10

LIVING RM. 21x21

B.R. 2

B.R. 3

WALKWAY

← TO PORCH PAVILION

MAIN LEVELS

(STREAM VIEWS)

Notice that the entrance is in the garage building, above. From there, a stair (around a dumbwaiter for handing bundles) led down to the living level, and then yet another stair led further down to the lowest level still some 30 feet in elevation above the level of the creek.

JACUZZI TUB

STALL SHOWER

(TUNNEL ABOVE)

SKYWELL OUTDOOR GARDEN

THERMAL BREAK (TYP.)

UP

SPIRAL STAIR IN ENCLOSURE

STORAGE

UNEXCAVATED

MASTER BED ROOM

HEATING AND AIR CONDITIONING

LOW CEIL'G

MASTER BED ROOM IS AT POOL LEVEL.

CLOSETS LINE B.R. HALLWAY

UP

LOWER LEVEL

And what a creek that is! Lined with huge old sycamores and dotted with boulders, it flows through a silent forest of old trees.

← WALKWAY TO SCREENED PAVILION

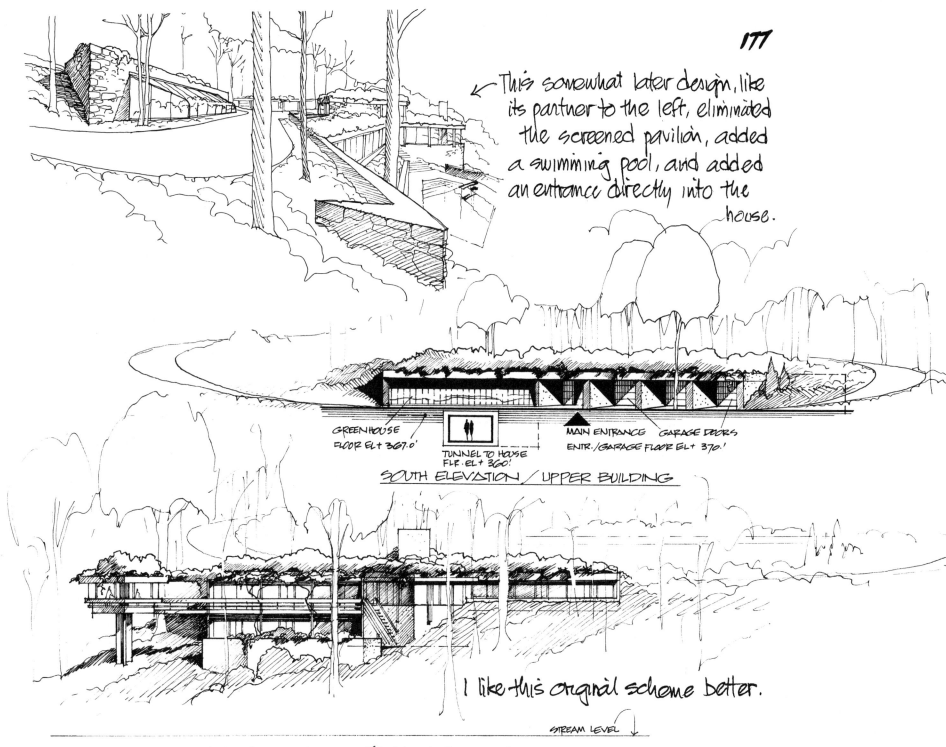

This somewhat later design, like its partner to the left, eliminated the screened pavilion, added a swimming pool, and added an entrance directly into the house.

GREENHOUSE
FLOOR EL+ 367.0'

TUNNEL TO HOUSE
FLR. EL+ 360'

MAIN ENTRANCE    GARAGE DOORS
ENTR./GARAGE FLOOR EL+ 370.'

SOUTH ELEVATION / UPPER BUILDING

I like this original scheme better.

STREAM LEVEL

SOUTH ELEVATION / LOWER BUILDING

This is one client I've got to identify.

Irvin Cohen has been such a good friend and client for so many years he's got to take a bow whether he wants to or not. He and his wife, Lois, let me design their house, back in 1963. Since then, he's had me design his office and factory at Wyomissing, Pennsylvania, and he's been willing to let me use many innovations in the additions he's built there. Solar heat, task lighting, earth cover, natural landscaping, percolation beds, exterior insulation... Here's another of those rare clients about which architects

dream. Mr. Cohen's latest addition to the Construction Fasteners complex was this earth covered parking lot entrance.

And now: a practice page ....

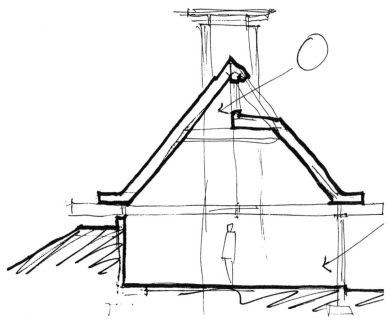

I shouldn't even think about big monster houses like this, especially for a single family, but I do love those long sweeping lines. Someday I'd like to do an earth-ridge house that looks like this. Would it live? Maybe it would if roots could be encouraged to grow thickly and survive during long dry periods.

Wouldn't it look great?

Refrigerating or freezing food is a big business today. (At Kansas City, abandoned mines that extend into hillsides, level, are easily kept at cold temperatures because of the lack of summertime warmth reaching them.)

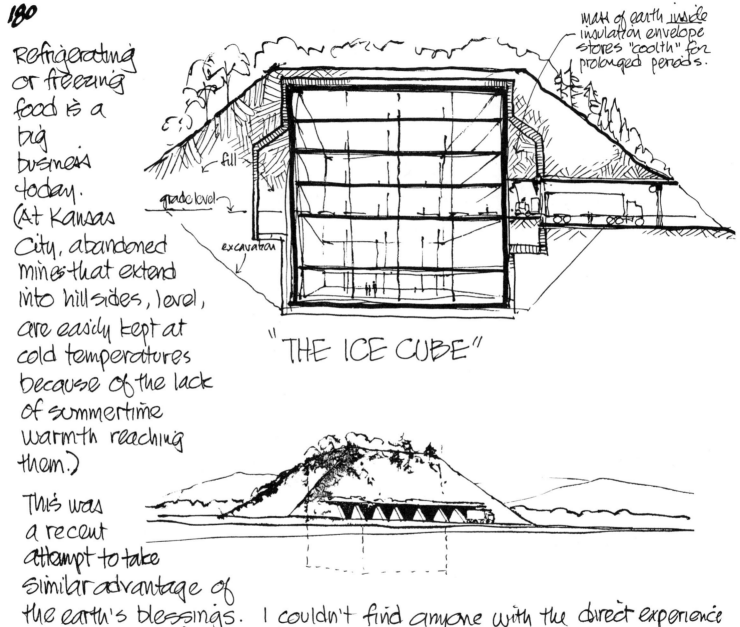

mass of earth inside insulation envelope stores "coolth" for prolonged periods.

fill

grade level

excavation

"THE ICE CUBE"

This was a recent attempt to take similar advantage of the earth's blessings. I couldn't find anyone with the direct experience and the credentials to advise me on the idea and again the momentum was lost with the client. It may still happen, though.

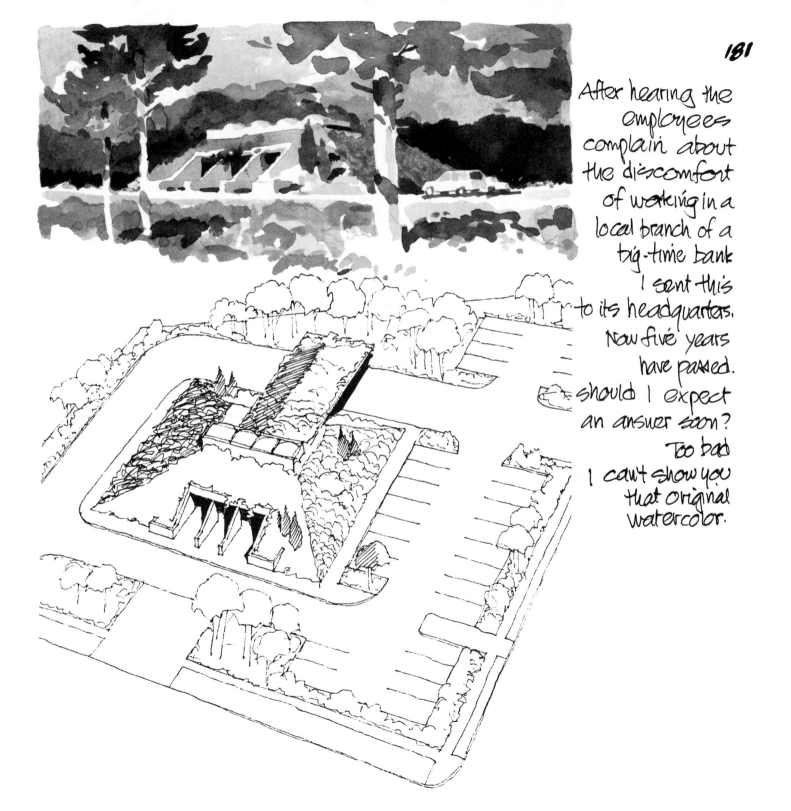

After hearing the employees complain about the discomfort of working in a local branch of a big-time bank I sent this to its headquarters. Now five years have passed. Should I expect an answer soon? Too bad I can't show you that original watercolor.

More miscellany...a proposal for a new →
church at Muncie, Pennsylvania, 1983;
a proposal for a new parish hall at a
Catholic Church here on Cape Cod;
← and the entrance to a house in Arkansas.

← This is the only one of the three
going ahead.

HEDGE CONCEALS
SUNKEN VEG.
GARDEN

TUNNEL
TO
OPEN,
WALLED
FLOWER
GARDEN

POROUS PAVING

EAST

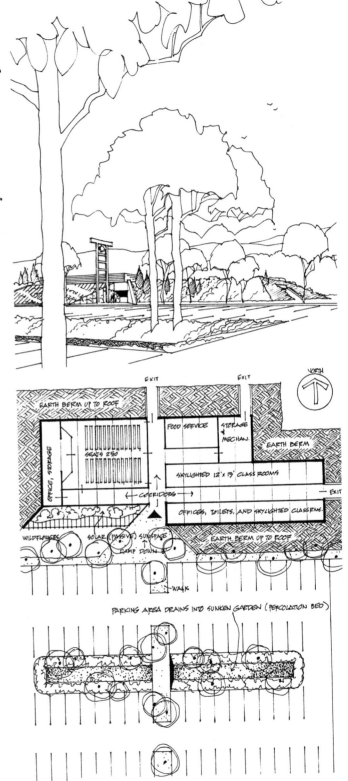

NORTH

EXIT          EXIT

EARTH BERM UP TO ROOF

FOOD SERVICE    STORAGE
                &
                MECHAN.            EARTH BERM

OFFICE, STORAGE    SEATS 250        SKYLIGHTED 12' x 15' CLASS ROOMS

← CORRIDORS →                                        ← EXIT

OFFICES, TOILETS, AND SKYLIGHTED CLASSRMS.

WILDFLOWERS    SOLAR (PASSIVE) SUNSPACE       EARTH BERM UP TO ROOF
               RAMP DOWN

WALK

PARKING AREA DRAINS INTO SUNKEN GARDEN (PERCOLATION BED)

Do I see seagulls flying <u>below</u>
an underground house? How I wish
I could! These people put
another damned Cape Cod
cottage on that beautiful
site.

This poolside house
isn't dead. Just
dormant. Why, it was
only 18 months ago
that I got that
gracious "we'll
be back" note
from the
owners.

April, 1989: Popular Science's editor was again kind enough to publish 2 designs of mine.... two designs for the same house! By rearranging the floor plans and the entrances a bit, I was able to adapt this by-now-familiar-to-you plan to work either way, making it suitable for almost any building lot big enough to accept it.

Northside entrance version

I sell construction plans, details, and specifications for either house (you must specify which one) for $100. In case you've forgotten, I am Malcolm Wells, Box 1149 Brewster, MA 02631.

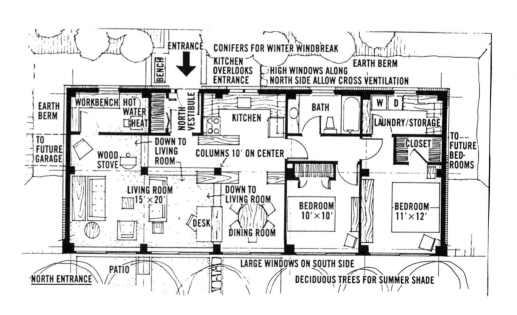

The perspectives look much better in color, of course. I'll try to remember to include them on the color pages.

*Southside entrance version.*

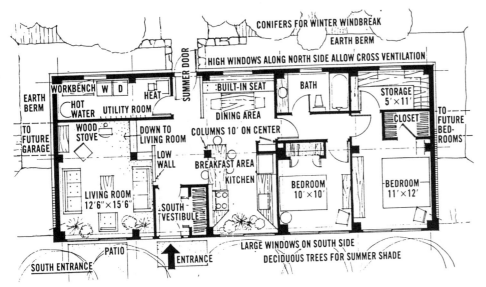

Notice that the house can be expanded very easily to either side... storage, bedrooms, garage, whatever.

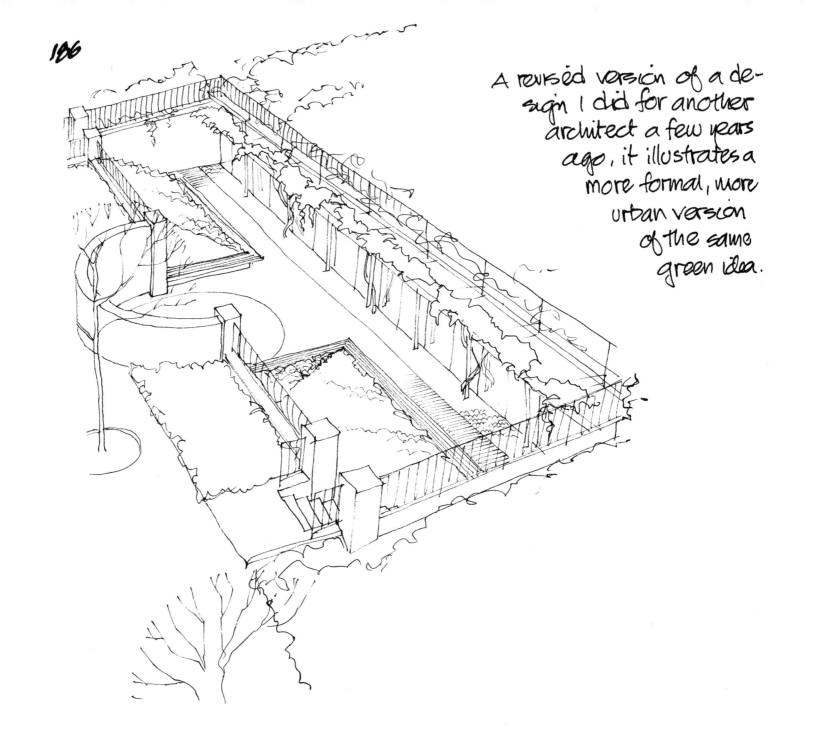

A revised version of a design I did for another architect a few years ago, it illustrates a more formal, more urban version of the same green idea.

The joint at the top of the wall in a buried building is always a problem. So many ~~many~~ materials come together there it's almost impossible to hope that all the water will be kept out. Sometimes I think the best solution is to raise the entire roof above the berm and let it act as a safety rail and drip ~~place~~ edge.

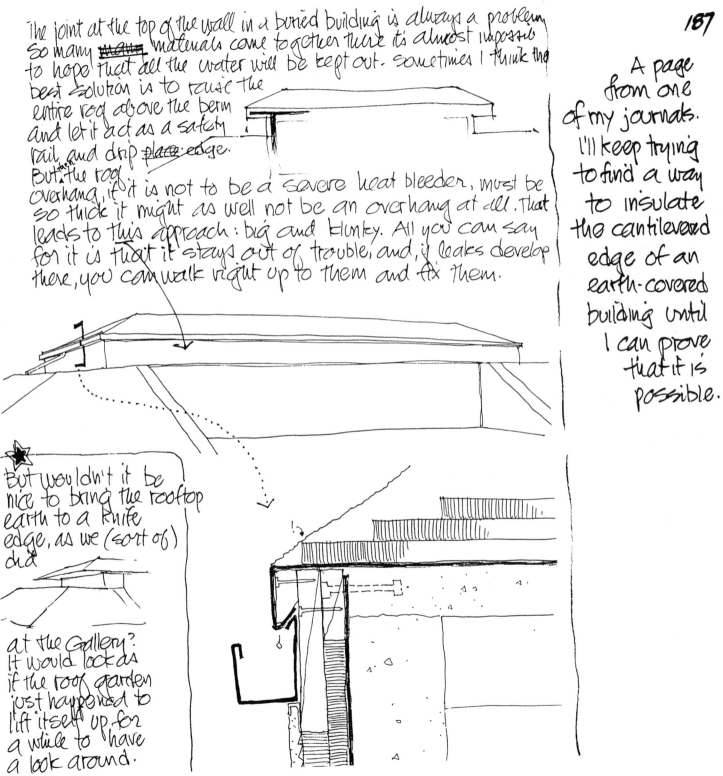

But the roof overhang, if it is not to be a severe heat bleeder, must be so thick it might as well not be an overhang at all. That leads to this approach: big and klunky. All you can say for it is that it stays out of trouble, and, if leaks develop there, you can walk right up to them and fix them.

A page from one of my journals. I'll keep trying to find a way to insulate the cantilevered edge of an earth-covered building until I can prove that it is possible.

But wouldn't it be nice to bring the rooftop earth to a knife edge, as we (sort of) did

at the Gallery? It would look as if the roof garden just happened to lift itself up, for a while to have a look around.

My most recent book is called <u>Classic Architectural Birdhouses and Feeders</u>*( CABAF, here in the office). Among its offerings is this "underground" birdhouse, high up on a pole. I built such a birdhouse, and was happy to see purple finches building a nest in it. The big haystack-shaped mound of grass thrived for a while but the drought caught up with it and by August the mound was golden, not green. That original mound had very little absorptive material inside. That's what led to the development of this water-holding version. It's bound to work a lot better but I haven't had a dry season yet in which to test it.

For a copy of this magnificent book, send me a mere $9.95 for a postpaid copy.

Do you still remember who I am, or must I tell one more time?

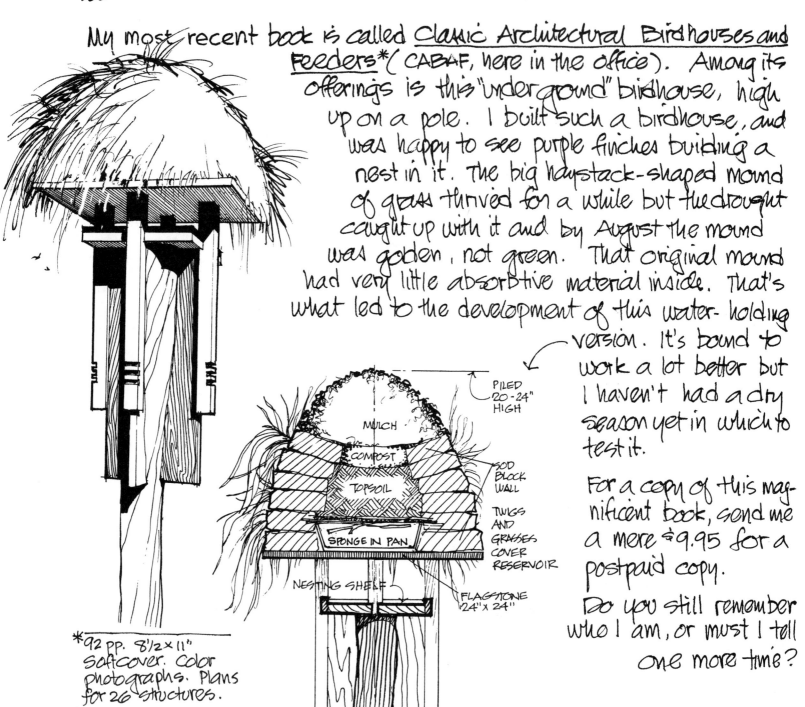

PILED 20-24" HIGH

MULCH

COMPOST

TOPSOIL

SOD BLOCK WALL

TWIGS AND GRASSES COVER RESERVOIR

SPONGE IN PAN

NESTING SHELF

FLAGSTONE 24" x 24"

*92 pp. 8½ x 11" Softcover. Color photographs. Plans for 26 structures.

# UNDERGROUND
## ARCHITECTURE
MALCOLM B WELLS ARCHITECT/CONSERVATIONIST
MONDAY NOVEMBER 29, 1971   7:30 P.M.
CRANBROOK ACADEMY OF ART   LECTURE HALL

Almost 20 years ago, a student I was never able to identify made this poster for my Cranbrook talk. Since then, I've used the upside-down-houses theme many times, most often in my Underground America Day notices. U.A. Day, by the way, is always on May 14th. Don't forget!

UNDERGROUND AMERICA DAY

And now a final note, as they say at the ends of newscasts: a house I'm just starting to design for a ridge-top site with an ocean view in northern California. The ridge, like that of the house on p. 94, runs north and south.

The End.

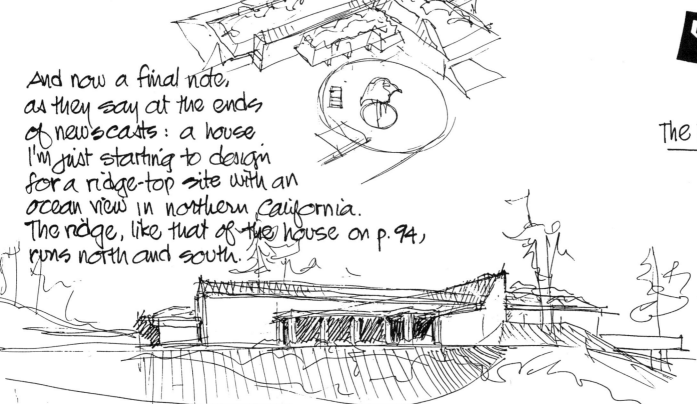

# The Real Goods Solar Living Books

*Wind Power for Home & Business: Renewable Energy for the 1990s and Beyond* by Paul Gipe

*The Independent Home: Living Well with Power from the Sun, Wind, and Water* by Michael Potts

*Real Goods Solar Living Sourcebook: The Complete Guide to Renewable Energy Technologies and Sustainable Living*, Ninth Edition, edited by John Schaeffer

*The Straw Bale House* by Athena Swentzell Steen, Bill Steen, and David Bainbridge, with David Eisenberg

*The Rammed Earth House* by David Easton

*The Real Goods Independent Builder: Designing & Building a House Your Own Way* by Sam Clark

*The Passive Solar House: Using Solar Design to Heat and Cool Your Home* by James Kachadorian

*A Place in the Sun: The Evolution of the Real Goods Solar Living Center* by John Schaeffer and the Collaborative Design/Construction Team

*Hemp Horizons: The Comeback of the World's Most Promising Plant* by John W. Roulac

*Mortgage-Free! Radical Strategies for Home Ownership* by Rob Roy

*The Earth-Sheltered House: An Architect's Sketchbook* by Malcolm Wells

Real Goods Trading Company in Ukiah, California, was founded in 1978 to make available new tools to help people live self-sufficiently and sustainably. Through seasonal catalogs, a periodical (*The Real Goods News*), a bi-annual *Solar Living Sourcebook,* as well as retail outlets, Real Goods provides a broad range of tools for independent living.

"Knowledge is our most important product" is the Real Goods motto. To further its mission, Real Goods has joined with Chelsea Green Publishing Company to co-create and co-publish the Real Goods Solar Living Book series. The titles in this series are written by pioneering individuals who have firsthand experience in using innovative technology to live lightly on the planet. Chelsea Green books are both practical and inspirational, and they enlarge our view of what is possible as we enter the next millennium.

Stephen Morris
*President, Chelsea Green*

John Schaeffer
*President, Real Goods*

## Other Books by Malcolm Wells

*Solaria,* with Harry Thomason and Bob Homan. Barrington, N.J.: Edmund Scientific Co., 1974.

*Energy Essays.* Barrington, N.J.: Edmund Scientific Co., 1974.

*How to Buy Solar Heating Without Getting Burnt,* with Irwin Spetgang. Emmaus, Penn.: Rodale Press, 1976.

*Underground Designs,* Self-published, 1977; $7.00.

*Notes from the Energy Underground.* New York: Van Nostrand Reinhold, 1979.

*Underground Plans Book I,* with Sam Wells. Self-published, 1980; $14.00.

*Sandtiquity,* with Connie Simo and Kappy Wells. New York: Taplinger Publishing Co., 1980. New edition forthcoming from Willow Creek Press.

*Gentle Architecture.* New York: McGraw Hill, 1981.

*Passive Solar Energy,* with Bruce Anderson. Amherst, N.H.: Brick House, 1982.

*The Children's Book of Solar Energy,* with Tilly Spetgang. New York: Sterling Publishing Co., 1984.

*Classic Architectural Birdhouses and Feeders.* Self-published, 1987; $2.24. Republished by Willow Creek Press, 1997.

*Underground Buildings.* Self-published, 1989.

*How to Build an Underground House.* Self-published; $12.00.

*The Successful Contractor.* Self-published, 1990; $6.00.

*Perspective.* Self-published, 1993; $12.00.

*Infrastructures.* Self-published, 1994; $16.00.

*Baseball Talk.* Self-published, 1994; $9.95. Republished by Willow Creek Press, 1997.

Self-published books with prices indicated are available postpaid from the author at:

Box 1149
673 Satucket Road
Brewster, MA 02631

# *Chelsea Green Publishing Company*

The sustainable world is one in which all human activities are designed to co-exist and cooperate with natural processes rather than dominate nature. Resources are recognized as finite. Consumption and production are carefully and consciously balanced so that all of the planet's species can thrive in perpetuity.

Chelsea Green specializes in providing the information people need to create and prosper in such a world.

Sustainable Living has many facets. Chelsea Green's celebration of the sustainable arts has led us to publish trend-setting books about organic gardening, solar electricity and renewable energy, innovative building techniques, regenerative forestry, local and bioregional democracy, and whole foods. The company's published works, while intensely practical, are also entertaining and inspirational, demonstrating that an ecological approach to life is consistent with producing beautiful, eloquent, and useful books, videos, and audio tapes.

For more information about Chelsea Green, or to request a free catalog, call (800) 639–4099, or write to us at P.O. Box 428, White River Junction, VT 05001. We invite you to visit our web site at www.chelseagreen.com.

In addition to the books listed on the opposite page, Chelsea Green's titles include:

| | |
|---|---|
| *The Man Who Planted Trees* | Jean Giono |
| *Beyond the Limits* | Donella Meadows, Dennis Meadows, and Jørgen Randers |
| *Loving and Leaving the Good Life* | Helen Nearing |
| *The New Organic Grower* | Eliot Coleman |
| *Solar Gardening* | Leandre Poisson and Gretchen Vogel Poisson |
| *Four-Season Harvest* | Eliot Coleman |
| *The Contrary Farmer* | Gene Logsdon |
| *Who Owns the Sun?* | Daniel Berman and John O'Connor |
| *Whole Foods Companion* | Dianne Onstad |
| *Gaviotas* | Alan Weisman |
| *The Book of Masonry Stoves* | David Lyle |

CHELSEA GREEN PUBLISHING CO.

# Index